STEPS TO
BETTER CHESS

7 STEPS TO BETTER CHESS

A GUIDE TO IMMEDIATELY MAKING YOU A BETTER PLAYER

ERIC SCHILLER

CARDOZA PUBLISHING

*This book is dedicated to all those who have taught me
lessons over the years, on and off the chessboard.*

Cardoza Publishing is the foremost gaming publisher in the
world with a library of more than 200 up-to-date and easy-
to-read books and strategies. These authoritative works are
written by the top experts in their fields and with more than
10,000,000 books in print, represent the best-selling and most
popular gaming books anywhere.

Copyright ©2010 by Eric Schiller
– All Rights Reserved –

Library of Congress Catalog No: 2010921135
ISBN: 1-58042-240-3
ISBN 13: 9781580422406
formerly titled Development of a Chess Master

Visit our website or write us for a full list of our
books, software and advanced strategies.

CARDOZA PUBLISHING
P.O. Box 98115, Las Vegas, NV 89193
Phone (800)577-WINS
email: cardozabooks@aol.com
www.cardozabooks.com

TABLE OF CONTENTS

Step 5: *Lessons in the Endgame*   101

Step 6: *Lessons Learned*   123

Step 7: *Final Thoughts*   189

♟ INTRODUCTION
The Lessons

Chess is a game where winning is a result of a mistake. If you don't make a mistake, you can't lose. In most games, both sides make a number of errors and the one who makes the last big mistake—leading to checkmate—loses. All chessplayers make mistakes. Even the great World Champions have managed to play some dreadful moves. Beginners naturally make a lot of mistakes, even accidentally losing pieces, but can often survive or even prevail, with a little help from the opponent. When facing stronger opposition, however, even a small error can lead to defeat. To make progress as a player, your number one task is to eliminate, or at least limit, your mistakes.

This book aims to investigate how bad moves can push past all the superior alternatives, and often lead to defeat. We'll look at typical mistakes as seen in my own games, hoping that you will learn from them and be able to avoid them in your own games. Many of these lessons were painful to me as a player. In most cases, I've been able to understand why the errors were made.

Although I can't say that all of them have been purged from my system, you'll see examples where I have overcome or avoided some common pitfalls. I'm confident that once you've worked through this book, your play will improve and you will be able to do without some of the painful experiences at the chess board that are a large part of the learning experience.

This book contains valuable lessons in every phase of the game. The seven steps to better chess are organized as follows:

1. LESSONS IN THE OPENING

The opening contains more danger than mere traps, as shown in our first chapter. The art of preparing for battle has been raised to new heights with universal access to chess computers and chess database software. Psychological preparation can be smashed by taking the game out of known paths – but how to know what the enemy knows? I learned a number of lessons in opening strategy and psychological preparation, which are shared here.

2. LESSONS IN BASIC TACTICS

This chapter deals with basic tactical errors, which plague top players as well as beginners. After all, in order to win a chess game, the opponent must make some kind of error. Without a serious mistake, the games are likely to end in draws. There are many reasons tactical errors are made, and half a dozen examples of psychological and other errors are presented.

3. LESSONS IN BASIC STRATEGY

The next chapter deals with strategic mistakes. Planning is one of the hardest chess tasks. Deciding whether or not the basis for an attack exists, or timing various positional moves, requires great care, and it is easy to slip up. A number of warning signs can be seen in the games analyzed in this chapter.

4. LESSONS IN THE MIDDLEGAME

The following chapter deals with middlegame lessons, with a baker's dozen of examples of middlegame play gone awry. Advanced strategy and tactics are seen here, together with many psychological mistakes. These were painful mistakes on my part, and I was duly punished for most of them. You can avoid this fate by keeping in mind the psychological traps that are likely to trip you up during the game.

5. LESSONS IN THE ENDGAME

We then reach the chapter on endgames. It took me a long time to even begin serious study of this critical stage of the game, as I explain at the start of the chapter. I have tried to make up for more-or-less ignoring the fundamentals of endgame play by devoting considerable study time to it over the past couple of decades. Just because I learned late doesn't mean you can't benefit now by avoiding my mistakes.

6. LESSONS LEARNED!

After witnessing all of these errors, you might be inclined to wonder how I could ever pull off an upset against my betters. The final chapter shows how I learned some lessons and applied them against top-flight competition. The games in this chapter aren't necessarily my best, but they are instructive wins over players rated from 2400 to 2650. Since my peak rating was 2370, they qualify as major upsets. Most of my opponents were Grandmasters, and with the exception of one simul game from my youth, all were played in tournaments with prize money at stake.

I hope that when you have finished playing over the games in this book you will have learned quite a lot and will make fewer mistakes in your own games. Perhaps the final chapter will help give you the confidence to play fearlessly against all opponents, no matter how high they are rated. Even the very best players are far from perfect, and in any case, if you do not make a mistake, they cannot defeat you!

7. FINAL THOUGHTS

I'll wrap the lessons up with some final advice and hopefully, send you on your way as a better chess player

BRIEF NOTES ON CHESS NOTATION

Each square can be described by combining the file and rank.. The horizontal rows of the board, called "ranks" are labeled a–h. The vertical columns of the board, called "files" are labeled 1–8. Each square can be described by combining the file and rank, To indicate a move, we start with the abbreviation of the piece being moved, as indicated in the chart below. If a pawn moves, we don't bother with any symbol.

K   King
Q   Queen
R   Rook
B   Bishop
N   Knight
Pawns   (omitted)

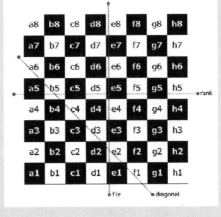

The abbreviation is combined with the square that the piece lands on. For example, if a bishop moves from f1 to b5, we write Bb5. When a piece makes a capture, an x is inserted between the first letter of the name of the piece in question and the destination square. For example, if the bishop had captured an enemy piece at b5, we write Bxb5.

When a pawn makes a capture, we indicated the file (but not rank) the pawn started on, followed by an x, and then the destination square. If the capture at b5 was made by a pawn on the c-file (at c4), instead of the bishop, we write cxb5..

Kingside castling is indicated by two zeroes separated by a dash: 0-0. Queenside castling is represented by three zeroes separated by dashes: 0-0-0. Check is indicated by a plus sign (+). Checkmate is indicated by the symbol #.

Chessplayers also use a set of symbols to express opinions on the position, or to point out special features. Cardoza Publishing prefers words, but we do adopt the standard suffixes to indicate the quality of a move, as in the following table.

!	Good move	??	Blunder
?	Bad move	!?	Interesting move
!!	Fantastic move	?!	Questionable move

♟ STEP ONE
Lessons in the Opening

Tactics are the building blocks of chess and when they fall, the game often falls with them. Tactical errors are more common among beginners but even the most skilled players drop pieces from time to time. World Champions have made tactical errors in the opening that have cost games in as little as a dozen moves. International Masters have dropped games in less than half a dozen moves. So, tactical errors will always be with us assuming my readers are human and not chess-playing computers!

Among accomplished players, a piece is not usually left hanging so that it can be captured in one move. Such errors are rare, and not particularly instructive. Losing a piece in two or more moves to a tactical trap or through an oversight is far more common. Double attacks and discovered attacks should be anticipated, but are often overlooked.

Let's start things off with a few blunders that are typical of amateurs, and trap a few masters, too!

FORGETTING ABOUT THE EDGES

When a piece or pawn is located on the edge of the board, and is not under attack, it is easy to forget about it. The item seems irrelevant, so no thought is given to it when grinding out analysis. It is easy for opponents, looking for targets anywhere on the board, to take advantage of such errors.

Position after 28.Bf3

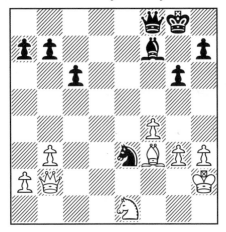

Pehnec vs. Schiller,
Manhattan Chess Club Tournament, 1971

28...Bd5? In trying to force pieces from the board and draw the game, I overlook the weakness of my pawn at a7.

GAME LESSON ONE

Never underestimate the weakness of pawns or pieces at the edge of the board!

29.Qd4! Bxf3? 29...Qe7 is strong, but easy to miss. It is natural to think defensively when two pieces are under attack, but, the merit of this move lies in the attack that will come if Black takes the a-pawn. 30.Qxa7? Nf1+; 31.Kg2 Qxe1; 32.Bxd5+ cxd5; 33.Qb8+ Kg7; 34.Qc7+ (34.Qxb7+ Kh6; 35.Qxd5 Ne3+) 34...Kh6; 35.g4 Qg3+!; 36.Kxf1 Qxh3+; 37.Kf2 Qxg4; Black is on top. **30.Nxf3 Nf5; 31.Qxa7.** White won the endgame.

PINS, FORKS AND OTHER OBJECTS OF TORTURE

Even World Champions make elementary tactical blunders from time to time, but in the following example, played recently, it is clear that I needed to spend more time checking for tactical traps. The pins, counter pins and final fork are quite elegant tactics in the hand of my master opponent, but I really should have seen them coming. Counterpins, where the pinning piece itself placed under a pin by the enemy are among the least obvious moves in chess. See for yourself and learn from this rich example so that you don't blow the win as I did.

Position after 22...Nf7

Schiller vs. Longren, Frisco Masters,
San Francisco, 2000

The game has been quite a battle. My king has been driven to h3, where it seems to be safe, and the pin at f7 should lead to the win of a piece. All I have to do is play 23.Qe7! However, I didn't see anything wrong with moving my queen to g4, where it attacks the pawn at d4. I figured that Bxd4 and Qxg7# was coming. It all seemed so simple at the time.

23.Qg4?? h5! Suddenly I realize that taking the pawn allows Black to equalize with a sac on g2, and a discovered attack on the bishop at e6. **24.Qg6?** Surely the queen is safer here than at f5? 24.Qf5! was correct, but I wanted to block the g-pawn, which might get my king into trouble.

It is remarkable that to avoid trouble on the c8-h3 diagonal I needed to bring my queen into the line of fire! Into the crossfire, in fact, as she is vulnerable on the f-file. At least I avoided 24.Qxh5?? Bg2+!!; 25.Kxg2 Qxe6.

24...Bd7!!

Position after 24...Bd7!!

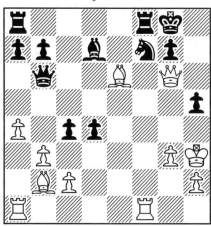

I didn't even consider this move, because I didn't realize the bishop was pinned. I had assumed I could always capture the knight with check, but Black's move pins the bishop on the diagonal. Ack!

25.Rae1 Bxe6+; 26.Rxe6. A rook is usually better than a bishop, but the rook here does not pin the knight, so...

GAME LESSON TWO

Make sure your pinning piece can't be counterpinned!

26...Ng5+!!; 27.Qxg5 Qxe6+. I resigned, because I'm going to lose the rook at f1 too. A very painful lesson in basic tactics, which I shouldn't need anymore.

THE ANALYSIS AIN'T DONE 'TILL YOU STICK A FORK IN IT

One of the easiest ways to get into trouble is to fail to analyze deeply enough. It is often difficult in a tournament, especially when the clock is counting down, to devote enough time to all the critical lines in a position. Some important variations may extend quite deep and it is easy to lose track. Mental discipline is required. The next game was played when I was a Class D player rated just over 1200. (How proud I was of the 1201 rating!)

Position after 24...Qe2

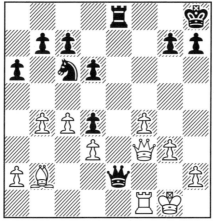

Schiller vs. Kiefer, National High School Championship New York City, 1970

25.Qxe2?! A very typical and instructive error. I didn't have the confidence to leave my bishop hanging and try 25.b5!

Qxb2; 26.bxc6. The pawn at c6 would be so weak after 16...
b6! That would have brought about a roughly level game.
    25...Rxe2; 26.Rf2? Simple miscalculation. It is true that I
will get the d-pawn if Black gets my c-pawn, but there is also
a fork of the pawns at a2 and d3. I should have played 26.b5!
Rxb2; 27.bxc6 bxc6; 28.Rf2. **26...Rxf2; 27.Kxf2 Nxb4;
28.Bxd4 Nxa2; 29.Ba7 Nb4; 30.Bb8 c6; 31.d4 d5; 32.cxd5
cxd5.** Black went on to win.

GAME LESSON THREE

When you have analyzed a position as deeply as
you can, try to go just a bit deeper!

LIBERATION AND REVOLUTION

    I did recover from the previous debacle and managed to
progress to the next level. The following battle of Class C
players shows that there was much yet to learn. Sometimes I
fell for the old trap of thinking that a pawn sitting on a square
prevents other pieces from using that square. If the pawn
moves, then I have time to defend, right?

    It doesn't work that way. If a player needs to use a square,
which is occupied by a piece, then the best tactic is to move
the piece while making a threat. Then the opponent doesn't
have time to react. In the next game I walk right into a punch
by giving my opponent the opportunity to clear a square with
an attacking move.

    You can avoid this problem by allowing your imagination
to examine scenarios where existing pieces are removed from
the board. This is a useful exercise, which can lead to spotting
many combinations. At the very least, it helps prevent the kind
of error seen in this game.

Position after 23.a4

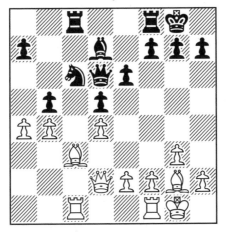

Jedzinak vs. Schiller, Quadrangular Tournament
Long Island NY, 1970

In this roughly level position, White creates problems for Black. The key to the position is the a3-f8 diagonal. Naturally since White has a blockaded pawn at b4, I didn't give it a thought. **23...bxa4?** After 23...Ne7! Black is not worse. **24.b5!** White's clearance sacrifice opened up b5, and now I can't avoid loss of material. **24...Ne7?** After my first error, I never recovered. Black's position was not lost until this move. 24... Nb8; 25.Bb4 Qb6; 26.Bxf8 Rxf8 is best. White will lose the b-pawn, so the position is only slightly better. **25.Bb4.** I resigned.

GAME LESSON FOUR

Remember that pieces that seem immobile can sometimes be moved after a preliminary maneuver.

THE OPPONENT IS NO DUMMY!

As in any sport, you need to respect your opponent! There is a danger when things go too well and you manage to get an advantage early in the game against an experienced and talented opponent. It is easy to become complacent, and assume that your opponent is going to continue to make mistakes. After obtaining a good position, you can be tempted to play ambitiously and boldly in positions that require patience and slow play.

Position after 19.Nd4

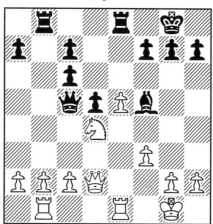

Minic vs. Schiller, Berlin Summer Open, Berlin, 1984

The opening had been going so well that I thought I had a clear win of a pawn here. It turns out to be a major tactical miscalculation! **19...Bxc2??** Retreating the bishop to g6 would have maintained equality. **20.Rbc1 Rb4.**

I had counted on this little tactic to put enough pressure at d4 to hold the position. **21.Red1!**

Position after 21.Red1

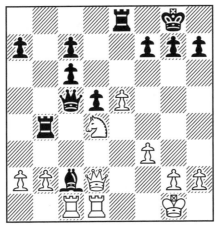

Oops! I forgot my own bishop was pinned. I have to exchange pieces and make the most of the situation. **21...Rxb2; 22.Rxc2 Rxc2; 23.Qxc2 Qxc2; 24.Nxc2.** The pawns don't make up for the missing knight. White had a clear advantage and went on to win.

The error here was one of disrespecting my IM opponent. Something should have told me he wasn't going to hang a pawn for nothing!

GAME LESSON FIVE

When things are going well against a strong opponent, be especially vigilant and check all tactics carefully!

KNOW ALL THE MATING POSITIONS!

There are not all that many types of checkmates, and it helps to know every one of them. Sometimes tragedy occurs when a winning position turns into a loss because of a type of checkmate that you haven't seen before.

That's the case in the next game, but had I not overlooked a basic trapped piece tactic along the way I wouldn't have needed to know it. The entire game is interesting and was widely published. We pick it up in the early middlegame, where I use a fine sacrifice to gain a winning position.

Position after 16.h3

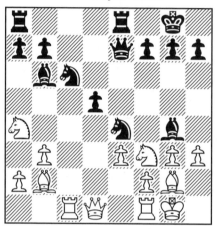

Meins vs. Schiller, Groningen GM Open
Netherlands 1996

This looks like a strong move since, if the bishop retreats, the power of the pin is lessened. Black, however, has other plans. On 16.Qxd5, I intended either 16...Nb4 or 16...Rad8. The former looked good to me during the game, but maybe it fails to a maniacally tactical line; 17.Qe5 Qxe5; 18.Nxe5 Bf5; 19.Bxe4 Bxe4; 20.Rc4 Nd3; 21.Rxe4 Nxb2; 22.Nxb2 f5; 23.Rf4 Rxe5; 24.Nc4 Rd5; 25.Nxb6 axb6; 26.a4 b5; 27.Rb4. White is clearly better.

16...Nxf2! A very strong sacrifice, which gives Black a definite advantage. **17.Rxf2 Bxf3.** The only correct continuation, since 17...Qxe3 fails to 18.Nxb6! and 17...Bxe3; 18.hxg4 is too much of an investment for Black. **18.Bxf3 Bxe3;**

19.Nc3 Qg5. There is no need to capture either rook when the bishop is so strong.

   20.Kg2 d4; 21.Nd5 Rad8.

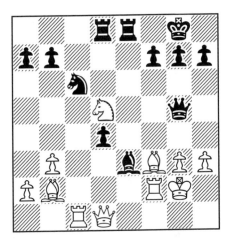

At this point I thought the game was simply winning, but White found a strong reply. **22.Rc5 Bxf2; 23.Kxf2 Ne5!** It took me far too long to work out the complications, and I caught up to my opponent on time. Each of us was down to 12 minutes for the remaining 17 moves. **24.Qxd4.** What a picture! White has veiled threats against g7 and the move Ne7+ must always be attended to. Black does not seem to have much of an attack, but in fact the attack continues. **24...Nxf3.** This undermines the knight at d5 and exposes the White king. Each of us is down to 8 minutes here. **25.Kxf3 Qf5+?!**

Wrong check. I missed the fact that the White knight is lost after ...a6 and ...b6, so that White cannot afford to exchange queens. On 25...Qh5+; 26.Qg4 Qxg4+; 27.hxg4 b6; 28.Rb5 a6; 29.Rxb6 Rxd5; 30.Rxa6 Rd3+; 31.Kf4 Rd2, Black wins. I must admit that I missed the entire line with ...b6 and ...a6. This would have been a much more efficient line, but my move should also win.

   26.Nf4 Rxd4; 27.Rxf5 Rd2; 28.Bc3 Rxa2; 29.Nh5 f6 Now 30.Bxf6 fails to 30...g6! **30.Rb5 Rd8; 31.Nf4 Rc2;**

32.Be1 b6; 33.h4 Rd1? This rook should have stayed home, but I didn't see any possible threat to my king. Extreme time pressure was forcing me to play quickly. **34.Bb4 Rf1+; 35.Kg4 g6; 36.h5.** Here all I had to do is play 36...Rb1, but with both flags hanging, I thought I saw a mating net. **36... Kg7?; 37.hxg6 hxg6; 38.Rd5.** Now things are tougher, because the simple 38...Rc7 fails to 39.Ne6+. Checking at f5 was necessary. **38...Kh6??** Now White forces mate, a pattern I have never encountered. I just never saw it coming. **39.Bf8+ Kh7; 40.Rd7+ Kg8; 41.Nxg6!**

Position after 41.Nxg6

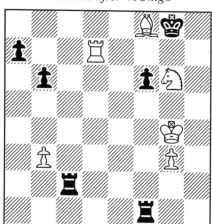

At first I thought I had won on time here, but I had forgotten to notate the exchange at g6. Then I thought that the position was not winning for me. Eventually, I realized it was lost because of the checkmate at g7.

GAME LESSON SIX
Study and learn all mating positions, even those that seem to be rare or improbable!

I had never seen this checkmating pattern, using bishop, knight and rook with no supporting king or pawns. Perhaps if I had a minute or two I might have figured it out, but my waste of time and poor decisions in the middlegame were the real culprits.

Mating positions should be part of your standard arsenal, and all checkmates need to be learned if you want to avoid a fate like this. One of my best games ever, and a major upset in full view of a lot of top professionals, ruined because of time trouble and ignorance!

♟ STEP TWO
Lessons in Basic Strategy

Strategic planning takes a long time to learn. While every beginner knows that the ultimate goal of the game is to checkmate the enemy king, it takes quite a while to understand the different demands of various stages of the game. What works well in the opening is not necessarily a good idea in the middlegame, and the endgame is in a universe of its own.

THE OPENING REVOLVES AROUND THE CENTER

The Fischer era did a lot of good for chess, but there was a downside for those of us who had no formal training or instruction. Fischer made hypermodern chess the norm, choosing defenses where Black that did not plant a firm stake in the center as the classical theorists were taught. Awash in Sicilians and King's Indians, we simply did not learn the importance of controlling the center. Sure, it was mentioned in some books, but other books proclaimed that center control was a silly old myth and that the Hypermoderns had disproved all that.

Well, the simple truth is: the center counts. Always did. It is just that the Hypermoderns opened up some ways of playing in the center without occupying it. That distinction was lost on me for a long time.

This is one of my most memorable games. In fact, it was memorable even before I played it, because I had a dream the night before that I would be playing the White side of this opening against Michael Wilder (who I lost to in the next round), and that I would get into trouble but find an ingenious way out.

This game was played in one of my most surprisingly successful tournaments, the 1979 New York City Championship. I was playing chess seriously for the first time in several years, and in the middle of the tournament, I had to drive down to Florida and fly back in time for the second weekend of play. Along the way, I studied the Caro-Kann, using it regularly for the first time, and it has remained a loyal friend to this day, after bringing me from a Class A player to a Master.

Lev Alburt went on to become the United States Champion. We became friends and wrote a book together on Lev's favorite Alekhine Defense. Meanwhile, here is the brutal, but not fatal, lesson I received at the board.

1.d4 Nf6; 2.c4 c5; 3.d5 b5; 4.a4. My old favorite against the Benko Gambit.

4...b4; 5.Nd2 d6; 6.e4 g6; 7.b3 Bg7; 8.Bb2 0–0.

Position after 8...O-O

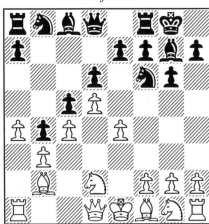

Schiller vs. Alburt, NYC Championship, New York, 1979

9.f4? This does not appear to be a bad move, but it leads to a lost position. 9.Bd3 was the logical move. **9...e5!** Ouch! If I capture at e5, then 10.Ng4! followed by 10...Nxe5 gives Black a great game. If I leave the pawn at f4, then Black captures and will soon occupy e5.

I must try to keep the e-file closed while my king is still in the center. **10.dxe6 fxe6.** I may have worries on the f-file, too. **11.g3.** OK, I'll get some play on the diagonals after all.

11...e5! Oh no! My understanding of play in the center was still very poor. **12.fxe5?** Thoroughly rattled, I make things even worse. If I feared this position with f-pawns still on the board, imagine my horror now!

12...Ng4!

Position after 12...Ng4!

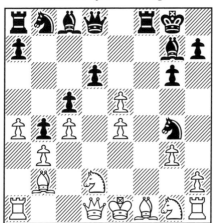

It's hopeless, I thought, as I tried to decide between 13.Ngf3, the obvious move, and 13.Qe2, getting ready to castle to the relatively safe queenside. Then a ray of hope appeared in the form of a strange choice. **13.Ndf3!** A truly remarkable move, because it is going to be very difficult to develop the kingside.

I have ideas for using the d2-square, which will become clear later. **13...Bb7; 14.Bh3 h5.** As expected. 14...Nxe5; 15.Bxe5! Bxe5; 16.Nxe5 is complicated, but White is in the game after either capture, or 16...Qe7.

15.Qe2 Qe7; 16.Bxg4! 16.exd6 Qxd6; 17.Bxg7 Kxg7; 18.Rd1 Qf6. Black is in serious trouble.
16...hxg4; 17.Nh4.

Position after 17.Nh4

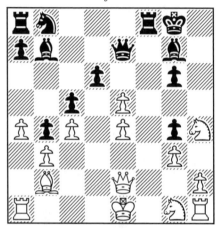

Finally, some counterplay in the form of a threatened fork at g6. My kingside is still paralyzed, but there are no immediate dangers. **17...Qg5; 18.Rd1.** Here the Grandmaster slips up. The correct plan, not easy to find, is to bring the knight into the game, and pave the way for the rook in the corner to join the fray. **18...Bxe5?!; 19.Bxe5 Qxe5; 20.Nxg6 Qxe4; 21.Nxf8 Kxf8.**

Position after 21...Kxf8

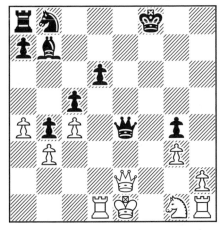

The position still seems to be hopeless for White. Exchanging queens leads to disaster on the light squares, on either side of the board. But I found a clever way to complicate the game by using the d2-square, as planned. **22.Kd2! Qd4+.** 22...Qxe2+; 23.Nxe2 Bxh1; 24.Rxh1 Nc6; 25.h3 is certainly no worse for White! **23.Kc2 Qc3+** Black will vacuum the queenside pawns. **24.Kb1 Qxb3+; 25.Kc1 Qc3+; 26.Kb1.**

Position after 26.Kb1

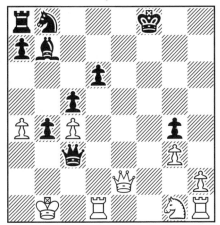

Black has a bishop and pawn for the rook, but can capture at h1. Or can he? **26...Nd7!** 26...Bxh1; 27.Rf1+ Bf3!; 28.Nxf3 Qb3+. Black can do no better than draw. **27.Qe6 Nf6; 28.Qxd6+.**

Position after 28.Qxd6+

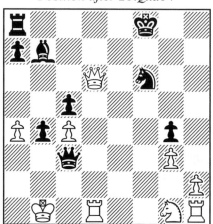

Black should still be winning, but needs to put the king on the right square. **28...Kg7??** 28...Kg8!; 29.Qe6+ Kh8 and White runs out of checks. **29.Qe7+ Kh6** or 29...Kh8; 30.Qxb7 and sooner or later Black must take the draw. **30.Rd6.** Now Black had no choice but to split the point. **30...Qb3+; 31.Kc1 Qxc4+; 32.Kb2.** Draw agreed.

There are a few lessons to be learned from this game. On the plus side, I did manage to find an escape route for the king and never gave up the fight, no matter how badly things looked. However, I allowed the game to open up before securing my king, and that should have cost me the game.

GAME LESSON SEVEN

Take care to keep your center strong until after you castle.

DON'T STOP ANALYZING WHEN YOU WIN MATERIAL!

When calculating variations, you need to know how deep to examine each line. In the first pass at a position, it is very easy to discard lines where you pick up a piece. After all, the opponent isn't going to go into a line that gives away a whole piece! There are some positions, however, where a variation leading to a win of material is deceptive. It is so easy to just stop analyzing when the variation grabs the piece, but if you do, there may be a nasty surprise at the end.

This isn't the same as considering an opponent's possible sacrifices. Whenever your opponents play leads to an obvious material loss, you are naturally suspicious. But when the position is buried a few moves into the analytical stream, you tend not to think of it as a sacrifice. In the game below, that's just what I did. Although objectively my position remained fine, psychologically my failure to consider my opponent's entire strategy added a lot of pressure, which in turn lead to enough bad decisions to cost me the game.

In this game, I hadn't managed to castle but wasn't too worried because my king has plenty of defense. I had ambitions on the kingside, but felt the need to open up the game for my bishop at b7 so that it could participate in an attack on the enemy king.

Position after 23.Bd3

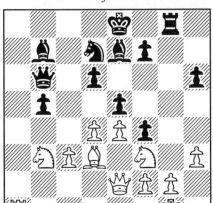

Delange vs. Schiller, Gausdal International
Norway, 1984

Black's king is a sorry sight. I really shouldn't be thinking about opening up the center, but that's the only arena available. The rook stares menacingly down the g-file, but it only serves to support some cheap threats at f3 or h3.

23...d5!?

I just couldn't find anything better. I saw the game continuation through move 26, but unfortunately missed White's shot on move 27. Still, the alternatives did not impress. 23...f5; 24.exf5 Qc6. The dual threats of Qxf3 and Qxc3 lead to recovery of the pawn. White still has the advantage. 25.Nbd2 Qxc3; 26.Ra7.

Also unappealing was 23...b4; 24.cxb4 Qxb4; 25.Rb1 with an unpleasant position for Black.

24.Nxe5 Nxe5; 25.dxe5 Kf8; 26.Qf3 Rg3.

Position after 26...Rg3

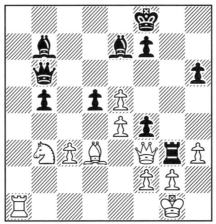

I figured that after the queen retreats, I just push the f-pawn to f3 and should clean up. One mistake is in not realizing the critical nature of the position and devoting sufficient time to analyzing a forced variation.

Another is underestimating, back at move 23, the weakness of the center and the power of the White e-pawns.

27.Qxf4! I didn't see this sacrifice coming. Well, I saw the move, but lazily stopped after mentally removing the bishop.

27...Rxd3; 28.e6! My opponent simply shoves the e-pawns down my throat, one after the other, until my position chokes.

28...Qxe6; 29.Nd4.

Position after 29.Nd4

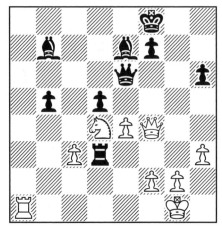

At this point I still had half an hour left for a dozen moves, plenty of time. I should have spent a lot of time choosing between c8 and d6 as destinations for my queen. My scoresheet shows that I only thought for a couple of minutes.

29...Qd6?

This move looks fine, but turns out to be bad. I should have chosen the other retreat. 29...Qc8; 30.Qxh6+ Ke8; 31.Qh8+ Kd7; 32.Qxc8+ Kxc8; 33.exd5 Rxc3; 34.Nxb5 Rc5; 35.Na7+ Kc7; 36.Nc6 Bxc6; 37.dxc6 Kxc6; 38.Ra7 Rc1+; 39.Kh2 Bd6+; 40.g3 Bc7. Black has an extra piece but will have a hard time keeping his remaining pawn. In any case, this is better than the game!

30.e5 Qg6; 31.e6!

Position after 31.e6

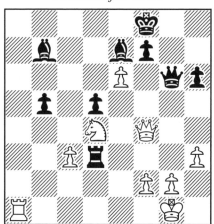

I spent half of my remaining half hour on this turn, mostly trying to work out what happens if I take the c-pawn. Instinct, rather than concrete analysis, led me to retreat. My opponent had over an hour left and I was beginning to get nervous. **31...Bc8?** 31...Rxc3 was correct. I should have taken the pawn, and guarded the c-file. 32.Qb8+ Bc8; 33.Nxb5 Rc4; 34.Nc7! Qf6; 35.Qxc8+ Bd8 (35...Kg7?? gets clobbered by 36.Ne8+); 36.e7+! (Not 36.Ra8?? Rc1+; 37.Kh2 Qf4+; 38.g3 Qxf2#). 36...Qxe7; 37.Ra8 Kg7; 38.Qxd8 Rc1+; 39.Kh2 Qxc7+; 40.Qxc7 Rxc7; 41.Rd8 Rc2! with a likely draw. **32.Qc7! Bxe6; 33.Ra8+ Kg7; 34.Qxe7 Rd1+; 35.Kh2 Qf6??** My time was down to mere seconds, and the game was in any case lost. 35...Rxd4; 36.cxd4 Kh7 gets blasted by 37.Qd8 Qg7; 38.Rb8.

GAME LESSON EIGHT
Remember that material advantage is only one part of the game.

36.Rg8+. I resigned, since after capturing the rook, the queen falls.

IS IT TIME TO ATTACK YET?

Attacking comes naturally to any chessplayer, especially when facing a higher rated opponent. In the next game I am facing a formidable opponent and one who was trained in Russia, so possessing considerably more technical prowess than most of the competitors. Not wanting to be ground down during a marathon game, I naturally chose an active opening. I play a move, which seems to take the initiative, but boomerangs because it only succeeds in improving the opponent's position.

1.Nf3 f5; 2.g3 b6; 3.Bg2 Bb7; 4.0–0 Nf6; 5.c4 c5; 6.Nc3 e6; 7.b3 Be7; 8.Bb2 0–0; 9.d4.

Position after 9,d4

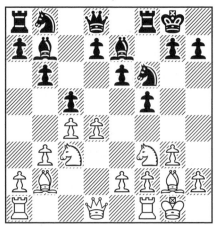

Zaltsman vs. Schiller, NYC Championship, NYC, 1979

9...cxd4?! I could not resist the temptation to lure the White queen to the center and then gain a tempo by attacking it with my bishop. I could have equalized with the sensible 9... Ne4!

10.Qxd4 Bc5; 11.Qf4.

Position after 11.Qf4

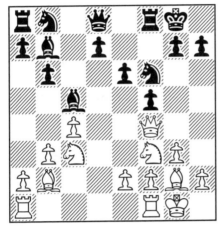

11...Nh5?! I rely on an attack with ...f4. But White has a solid defensive formation, so perhaps 11...Nc6 would have been wiser. **12.Qd2 f4; 13.Na4 fxg3; 14.hxg3.**

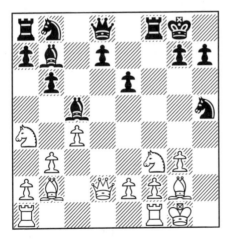

I had spotted the pin on the f-pawn but overestimated the effect of the capture at g3, since the bishop is under attack.

14...Bxf3. 14...Nxg3; 15.Nxc5 Bxf3 was the alternative. What a mess to have to deal with at the board. The complications

continue, but White comes out on top. 16.Nxe6! dxe6 (16...
Nxf1; 17.Qd4!); 17.Qxd8 Rxd8; 18.Bxf3 Nxf1; 19.Bxa8 Nd2;
20.Bg2.

White has the bishop pair and better pawn structure.
Black's outside passed pawn would not have been sufficient
compensation.

15.Bxf3 Rxf3; 16.exf3 Nxg3; 17.Rfe1 Qh4.

Position after 17...Qh4

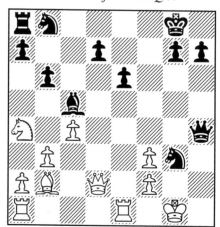

This line was much easier to calculate and I figured I
would have a very strong attack. The problem that I overlooked
was the horrible lack of development on the queenside. This
reinforces the idea that my 11th move was misguided.

I was also so taken with my attack on the h-file that I
totally forgot that the h7-square would be vulnerable. As the
game shows, it is White who takes advantage of the h-file.

18.Kg2 Nh5; 19.Re4! So much for my ambitions at f4! If
only the rook at a8 were at f8.

19...Qe7; 20.Nxc5 bxc5; 21.Rh1.

Position after 21.Rh1

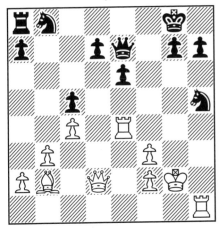

Black's position is already hopeless. **21...Nf6; 22.Qg5 Nc6; 23.Bxf6! Qxf6; 24.Qxf6 gxf6; 25.Reh4 a5; 26.Rxh7 Ra7; 27.Rh8+ Kg7; 28.R1h7+.** White eventually won.

GAME LESSON NINE

Keep in mind that when you open up the game, your opponent has more mobility, too.

DO NOT PUT OFF UNTIL NEXT MOVE THAT WHICH CAN BE DONE RIGHT AWAY!

In the next position, I have the opportunity to radically change the game by capturing at f3. My decision was to refrain from opening up a big b1-h7 diagonal for my opponent, thinking that it would therefore remain forever closed, except under the most favorable of circumstances. It turns out that the most favorable circumstances were right there on the board, and the moment to act was now! After letting the opportunity slip, I don't get another chance.

The lesson here is that you have to work extra hard in "critical positions," where the nature of the game can be changed radically. As we have seen, it is a mistake to open things up prematurely, but no less an error to delay when the active move is the correct one.

Perhaps the best advice I can give is that you should think with a positive attitude. Ask yourself, "Can I get away with this?" rather than "What can happen to me if I open up the game?" while allowing yourself extra time to ponder the position. Taking ten percent of your total time is reasonable, and even more if the position is very complicated.

Position after 24.Re1

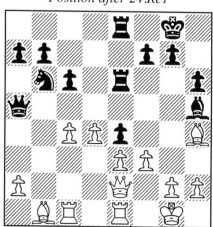

Finegold vs. Schiller, Midwest Masters, Chicago, 1984

I have typically made more errors in good positions than bad ones. I've got a great game here, but my next move is a turkey.

24...Qa3?! Why not just win material? The move is too ambitious, hoping the pressure on e3 will be too great. The flaw in my thinking clearly involved failure to appreciate the dangers along the b1–h7 diagonal.

After 24...f5; 25.Bf2, White could defend without difficulty. 24...exf3!, however, is another matter. 25.gxf3 Rxe3; 26.Qxe3 Rxe3; 27.Rxe3 f6! I missed this defensive resource, which protects e8. Black has a queen and pawn for two rooks, and more White pawns are likely to fall. I'm not sure if Black's advantage is winning, but it is indisputable.

25.Qc2! f5. Too late to capture now! 25...exf3??; 26.Qh7+ Kf8; 27.Qh8#.

26.f4 Bf7; 27.Qb3 Qa6. So much for my attack. The position is now objectively about even, but it was hard for me to come up with a coherent plan. I hadn't rebounded from the psychological effects of my decision at move 24. **28.a3 Rg6; 29.Ba2 Na4; 30.Qc2 Nb6; 31.Qc3 Na4.**

Having let the advantage slip, I was not opposed to a draw.

32.Qb4. White does not retreat. After all, the two bishops are worth something.

32...b6; 33.Qd2 Rc8; 34.Bb3 b5; 35.Qb4 Rg4; 36.cxb5 cxb5; 37.Bxf7+ Kxf7; 38.Qb3+. White threatens to trade rooks and grab the b-pawn, so Black has to block.

38...Rc4!; 39.Bg3 h5; 40.Re2.

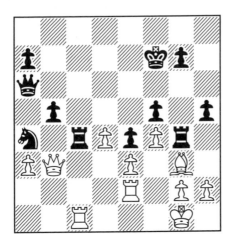

I've managed to hold my own, and there is nothing wrong with the position. However, the end of time control is always dangerous territory. I decided to break the pin and get my king to safety, but in doing so I lock my rook at g4. **40...Kg6?** Better was 40...h4; 41.Be1 h3; 42.g3 Nb6; 43.Rb1 Nd5!? I missed this shot during the game. 44.Qxb5 Qxb5; 45.Rxb5 Ke6. White is better, but the knight is more valuable than the bishop and White's extra pawn is blockaded. This would have been better than the game.

GAME LESSON TEN
Seize the moment!

41.Rec2 Rxc2; 42.Rxc2 b4!? Black's position is worse than it looks, as the following variations show. So I try to open a line for my queen. If 42...Kh7; 43.Qd5 Qg6; 44.Rc8! White has an elegant win. 44...Nb6; 45.Qg8+ Kh6; 46.Qh8+ Qh7; 47.Rc6+ Rg6; 48.Qd8! I wasn't going to fall for 42...h4; 43.Qd5 Kh7; 44.Rc6 Qxc6; 45.Qxc6 hxg3; 46.Qxb5 with an easy win for White.

43.axb4 Kh7; 44.Ra2 h4; 45.Rxa4 Qg6; 46.Rxa7 hxg3; 47.h3. What a horrible place for a rook! **47...Qc6.** Perhaps my opponent will overlook a back rank mate? **48.Ra1.** No such luck. I held out another dozen moves before White won.

OVERLY OPTIMISTIC SACRIFICE

Parting with the lady is a lot of fun at the chess board, if not in real life. Queen sacrifices are among the most accessible items of chess art, and I try to play them when the opportunity seems ripe. In a number of cases, the temptation to create a work of art can override common sense itself as the following game shows. You must not allow yourself to be seduced by a beautiful move, because the consequences can be severe indeed.

Position after 17.Qe1

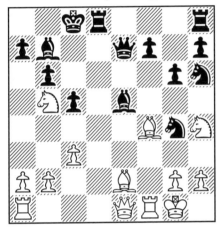

Loscutoff vs. Schiller, People's Open, Berkeley, 1997

17...Bxf4?? All I had to do was play the obvious 17...a6. Black is clearly better. But I decide to sac the queen for two pieces, a pawn or two, and an attack. **18.Bxg4+ Nxg4; 19.Qxe7 Bxh2+; 20.Kh1 Rhe8; 21.Qg5 f5; 22.Nxf5! h5.** I couldn't capture at f5. 22...gxf5; 23.Qxf5+ Rd7; 24.Nxa7+ Kd8; 25.Qxg4 and White wins. **23.Nh4 Bg3; 24.Nxg6 Kb8; 25.Rf7 a6; 26.Na3 Rd3; 27.Nf4 Rde3; 28.Nxh5.**

I suppose I could have resigned with only half the material I need to make up for the missing queen. However, White's king is not safe, so I try a few tricks.

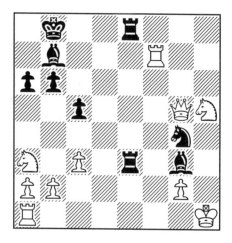

Amazingly, these few tricks salvage a draw!

28...Nf2+. 28…Re1+ is easily handled by 29.Rf1. **29.Rxf2 Bxf2; 30.Qf4+ Ka7; 31.Qxf2.** White has won two pieces for the rook, but the pin on the g-pawn gives me a fork which picks up the knight at h5. **31...Rh3+!; 32.Kg1 Rxh5; 33.Re1 Reh8; 34.Qf4 Rh4; 35.Qe3 Rh2; 36.Qg3 Rh1+; 37.Kf2 Rf8+; 38.Ke2 Re8+; 39.Kd2 Rhxe1; 40.Qxe1 Rxe1; 41.Kxe1 Bxg2; 42.Nc2.**

Draw agreed.

GAME LESSON ELEVEN

A win is more important than a brilliancy prize!

♟ STEP THREE
Lessons in Basic Tactics

I always advise my students to castle as soon as there is daylight between the king and rook, unless there is an immediate win available. Setting aside castling in favor of some other move is an integral component of some advanced opening strategies, but in general, if you don't castle, sooner or later it will come back to bite you. All my students know this, though they aren't perfect in their execution. Perhaps they are following my dubious example, as from time to time I still get into trouble because my king safety is not my own top priority.

Even prepared openings have to take care to watch for king safety, and there are some other speed bumps that must be taken seriously. Many are psychological. Some people wonder, quite legitimately, why someone who has done so much opening analysis as author, trainer, second and commentator could possibly fall apart early in the game. I wish I knew the answer! Most of the time, the problem arises from an irrepressible improvisational streak.

You should stick to your opening preparation unless you see something at the board that gives you some reason to reconsider your analysis.

In most cases it is better to play your prepared move, and trust your preparation. If it doesn't work out, you can repair the problem at home where you can devote time and resources to the project.

The other lessons in this chapter include insuring that you take into consideration alternative plans for your opponent so that you aren't confronted by unexpected novelties early in the game – and the need for patience.

CASTLE!

Castling is critical for king safety. Just do it. Because when you don't, there's trouble ahead. And if the enemy has a rook on the e-file, castle quickly, because a clogged file can be unplugged quite rapidly, especially if the e-pawns are no longer on their home squares.

Position after 15...Rae8!

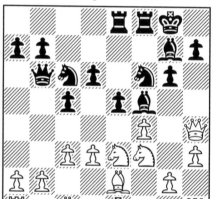

Schiller vs. Norwood, NatWest Young Masters
London, 1986

Fifteen moves into the game, my king is still in the center. I can kingside castle at will, which is some justification for allowing other moves to come first. At this point, I should castle immediately, or after a capture at e5 and f5. I have four minor pieces defending the king, but the rook on e8 is ready to open fire! It is stunning how quickly the game falls apart.

16.g4? Bxd3!! I overlooked this. **17.Bxd3 exf4; 18.0–0.** Finally, but it is too late. **18...fxe3; 19.Ng5 d5.** Two pawns down, I couldn't save the game.

GAME LESSON TWELVE
Failure to castle is often a capital offense, and your king may lose his head as a result!

BE PREPARED!

Opening preparation is part of every player's experience. Even beginners usually have a sense of the first few moves they intend to play, even if it is as simple as meeting 1.e4 with 1...e5. When just starting out, it is enough to know that you should plant a pawn in the center, develop pieces, castle, and try to connect your rooks by removing any pieces that stand between them. That simple advice can keep you out of trouble, but as you progress you'll find that you need more specific preparation for a variety of enemy plans.

At the higher levels of chess, opening preparation can become compulsive, with hours and hours of study invested in finding a single good move which might not get played until after move 25, but for most players, such work is a waste of time as it is unlikely any opponent will follow some theoretical recommendation so deep into the game. How deeply you should prepare is the subject of the next lesson. In this game, you will see how it is difficult to come up with good moves when caught unprepared.

Here is a game in which the six-time US Champion demonstrates his originality in the opening, and strength in the middlegame. After a dubious exchange sacrifice, I am positionally lost. Damn swisses! No time to prepare. Five minutes with Najdorf meister, Danny Olim, and I would have raced into Browne's favorite defense, looking forward to an interesting theoretical duel.

Against a GM, mainline theory is the best plan. Use the mighty power of Grandmaster experiences to present the GM with the need to improve on existing theory, or sidestep it with an inferior line. But I couldn't walk into such a theoretical jungle without preparation, so I switched to the Reti (or so I thought), an opening which I would use during the next year to knock off two Grandmasters.

1.Nf3 d6.

A last chance for me to enter the labyrinth of the Sicilian with 2.e4, and I thought about it — for a split second. **2.d4.** Well, we may go into a Torre after 2...Nf6; 3.Bg5. I know a little something about that, having written books on it.

2...Bg4.

The Wade Defense took me by surprise. True, it is now a respectable opening, but still has an unorthodox flavor, which I thought was unappealing to Browne's rather conventional palate. I wasn't too unhappy, since I play the defense myself, and could at least choose a line, which made me a bit uncomfortable when I was on the Black side of the position.

3.c4.

At the board, I wondered what Grandmaster Tisdall would do? The expatriate American was my housemate for a while in England, and I recalled that he likes the plan with Qb3. When we were fiddling around with the position once I wasn't able to come up with a convincing counterplan. Why this entered my head, I do not know, but I didn't really consider the immediate e4, leading to main lines, which I enjoy as Black.

3...Nd7; 4.Qb3 Rb8.

Position after 4...Rb8

Schiller vs. Browne, Western States Open, Reno, 1997

Now we are getting weird. Or so I thought. I really should have been familiar with this position, as it should have been in my repertoire as Black. But my general opening preparation had a serious gap, and now I had to find a way to climb out of the hole and get to some sort of position that would not give my opponent an advantage.

5.g3. I felt the bishop would be useful at g2. Browne's move is by no means original, strange as it may appear. With White committed to the fianchetto, Black may be able to use a break with ...b5. There are plenty of alternatives, and perhaps hitting the bishop with 5.h3 is best.

5...g6; 6.Bg2 Bg7. 6...c5; 7.e3 Qa5+; 8.Nbd2 Bxf3; 9.Bxf3 Bg7; 10.Qd3 Ngf6; 11.0–0 0–0; 12.Bg2 b5; 13.b3 led to obscure complications in Olafsson-Kosten, Hastings 1990. I was unprepared for this line and was improvising. Had I been familiar with the prominent games I mention now in hindsight, I would have fared much better in the game.

7.Be3.

Now we are getting weird. Or so I thought. I really should have been familiar with this position, as it should have been in my repertoire as Black. But my general opening preparation had a serious gap, and now I had to find a way to climb out of the hole and get to some sort of position that would not give my opponent an advantage.

5.g3. I felt the bishop would be useful at g2. Browne's move is by no means original, strange as it may appear. With White committed to the fianchetto, Black may be able to use a break with ...b5. There are plenty of alternatives, and perhaps hitting the bishop with 5.h3 is best.

5...g6; 6.Bg2 Bg7. 6...c5; 7.e3 Qa5+; 8.Nbd2 Bxf3; 9.Bxf3 Bg7; 10.Qd3 Ngf6; 11.0–0 0–0; 12.Bg2 b5; 13.b3 led to obscure complications in Olafsson-Kosten, Hastings 1990. I was unprepared for this line and was improvising. Had I been familiar with the prominent games I mention now in hindsight, I would have fared much better in the game.

7.Be3.

Position after 7.Be3

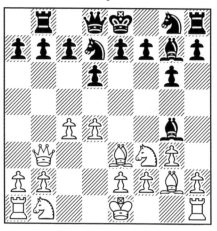

7...Nh6. 7...c5 can be played immediately, and usually play transposes. 8.Nbd2 Nh6; 9.dxc5 Nxc5; 10.Bxc5 dxc5; 11.0–0 0–0; 12.Ne4 Qa5; 13.Rfd1 b5!; 14.Nxc5 Rfc8; 15.Nd7 bxc4 forces White to accept a miserable game after 16.Qe3 Nf5 or go for broke here. 16.Qxb8 Rxb8; 17.Nxb8 Bxb2; 18.Nc6

Qa4!; 19.Rab1 c3 and Black won without difficulty in Scarella vs. Bezold, 1992 World Junior Championship. But my next move takes the game into new territory.

8.Ng5?! I wanted to try to trap the bishop. 8.Nbd2 c5 leads to the previous note.

8...c5! 8...Nf5; 9.h3 Nxe3; 10.Qxe3 Bf5; 11.Nc3 was what I had in mind. **9.dxc5 Nf5!** 9...Qa5+; 10.Bd2 Qxc5; 11.h3 Bf5; 12.e4 Be6; 13.Nxe6 fxe6 struck me as a position with more potential for White.

10.h3.

Position after 10.h3

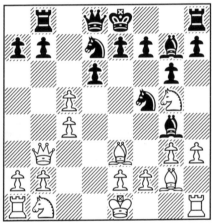

I decided to sacrifice the exchange at a1, hoping to mount an attack that never really materializes. 10.cxd6 Nxe3; 11.Qxe3 Bxb2 is also nothing for White. For example, 12.Bd5 e6; 13.h3 Bxa1; 14.hxg4 Qa5+; 15.Nd2 Qc3! **10...Nxe3; 11.Qxe3 Bxb2; 12.hxg4 Nxc5; 13.Qf4 f6; 14.Nxh7 Bxa1; 15.Nd2 Qa5; 16.Bd5 Kd7; 17.Kf1 Be5; 18.Qe3 Qc3!**

Position after 18...Qc3

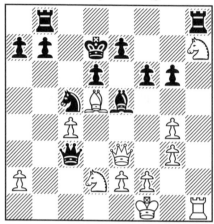

White is already lost. Left to my own devices against a Grandmaster, I was unable to carry out the opening phase of the game properly and went down to defeat at move 40.

GAME LESSON THIRTEEN

Make sure you are prepared for all reasonable replies to the first few moves of the game!

PREPARE DEEPLY

In the previous game I was unprepared for my opponent's fifth move. In the next game the situation is quite different. We rattle off 18 moves of known theory. In the previous game, the result was determined by that move. In this one, I thought I knew what I was doing. In reality, I was blindly following a line I had learned without really exploring the final position.

That would be a forgivable sin if the published evaluation were an advantage for one side or equality, but the authorities had declared the position unclear. That imposes a responsibility on the player.

If the theoreticians opt out, you need to analyze it yourself or use a computer program, preferably both! Back in 1990, computers probably could not handle the complexities of the position. To be fair, this was a casual game with no preparation, but this was my main defense to the Italian Game at the time and I had spent many hours analyzing the 5...b5 lines, to which I had contributed an important novelty a decade back.

The lesson to be drawn from this game is that when you study an opening and find a position that is considered unclear, you have to dig deeper and try to make sure that it isn't actually lost! An evaluation of "unclear" indicates that you have work to do!

1.e4 e5; 2.Nf3 Nc6; 3.Bc4 Nf6; 4.Ng5 d5; 5.exd5 b5; 6.Bf1 Nd4; 7.c3 Nxd5; 8.Ne4 Qh4; 9.Ng3 Bg4; 10.f3 e4; 11.cxd4 Bd6; 12.Bxb5+ Kd8.

Position after 12...Kd8

Edwards vs. Schiller, Played Online, 1990

Both players were familiar with the latest theory of this fascinating line. At the time, both castling and developing the queen were being investigated. Now 13.O-O is the normal move, leading to positions considered favorable for White after Black captures on f3 and White then moves the queen to b3.

In the game, the alternative line with an immediate queen deployment was seen.

13.Qb3 Bxg3+; 14.Kd1 Be6; 15.Bc6 exf3; 16.Bxd5 fxg2; 17.Qxg3 Qxg3; 18.hxg3 Bxd5.

Position after 18...Bxd5

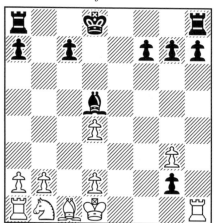

A known position, evaluated as unclear by Estrin. Black has 6 pawns, to White's 4.5 (the doubled d-pawn isn't worth much) and the strong protected pawn at g2 ads a bit more compensation for the knight. After playing this game, however, I became convinced the line is clearly better for White. Computer programs vary widely, some claiming White is clearly better, others preferring Black!

19.Rg1 Re8; 20.Nc3 Bf3+; 21.Kc2 g5!? The idea is to play ...h5-h4 and get my pawns connected. 21...Rb8 would have been wiser, but I doubt Black has enough for the piece after 22.d3 Rb6; 23.Bf4. **22.d3 f6; 23.Ne4!** All this might have been easy to find in preparation, and surely I would have known better than to play the simplifying **23...Bxe4?; 24.dxe4 Rxe4; 25.Rxg2 Rxd4; 26.Bd2.** I lost eventually. My dear bishop is gone, and the greatest hope, the pawn at g2, has been swept from the board.

What would my approach have been with proper study? I would surely have realized that after 23.Ne4!, the only serious try is 23...Rxe4; 24.dxe4 Bxe4, keeping the pawn at g2. At the moment, there are only two pawns for the rook, but White will probably return the rook for the bishop and pawn, emerging with an extra bishop in the endgame. So, the entire variation with 21...g5 would have been rejected, and some alternative would have been ready. If no good option exists, then Black would have to deviate earlier, or perhaps give up the entire line!

GAME LESSON FOURTEEN

If you are going to play popular lines which have been analyzed deeply, make sure you evaluate the final positions with special care if they are considered "unclear."

DON'T GET SEDUCED BY A PROMISING LINE!

Given all the available books and databases, it is a bit harder to get caught by a new move early in the game. That is, you won't get surprised if you spend substantial chunks of your life studying chess openings! For most players, these resources don't come into play. Openings are more easily learned from books with lots of prose than from encyclopaedic collections of thousands of games. So the particular danger exposed in the next game remains relevant to most chessplayers.

When you learn an opening there are often some clever lines that you'd love to see at the board. Authors usually go to great lengths to display these tricks, because it is part of giving the reader confidence in the opening. Sometimes, however, they lie buried in a little footnote. The observant reader spots

ERIC SCHILLER • CARDOZA PUBLISHING

the jewel, polishes it a bit by checking the conclusions of the author, and then sallies forth to slay some unwitting opponent with the discovery.

Sometimes it goes down as planned, but in other cases the attempted hijacking of a point is foiled because the path leading up to the brilliant move wasn't scouted properly. From a psychological standpoint, this is easy to understand. You really want the line to work, and look forward to the congratulations you will receive when the trap is sprung.

The prepared line doesn't have to lead to a forced win, but will deliver a superior position while humiliating the ignorant opponent. You don't really want to find a flaw in the moves leading up to the surprise, do you?

Well, in chess you have to be objective. I learned a painful lesson at the hand of a strong veteran International Master who had contributed many new moves to opening theory over the years. I assumed he would just follow a famous game in a variation which almost all the books indicated was great for Black. My surprise was hidden in a little footnote in a detailed monograph. Before I had a chance to play it, my opponent sprung a surprise of his own.

To avoid this disaster, make sure that your opening preparation considers all reasonable options for the opponent. Do not concentrate solely on the most interesting or complicated line.

Let's see what happens in this next game.

1.d4 Nf6; 2.Nc3 d5; 3.Bg5 Nbd7; 4.f3 c6; 5.e4 dxe4; 6.fxe4 e5; 7.Nf3.

Position after 7.Nf3

Schiller vs. Ligterink, Reykjavik Grand Open
Iceland 1986

I had prepared this move as an alternative to the capture at e5, seen in a well known Mikhail Tal game. I had known Tal since the 1980 Olympiad and he was taking a glance at each of my games during the Icelandic tournament, and offered me advice after each game. I'll always be grateful for his friendship, especially since he was, with Fischer, my idol when I was learning the game.

Take a look at the game Alburt vs. Tal, from the 1972 Soviet Championship, which is often cited as a reason White's whole opening strategy is ineffective. 7.dxe5 Qa5; 8.exf6 Qxg5; 9.fxg7 Bxg7; 10.Qd2 Qxd2+; 11.Kxd2 Nc5; 12.Bd3 Be6; 13.Nf3 0–0–0; 14.Ke2 b5; 15.a3 a5; 16.h3 Rhe8; 17.Rhd1 f5!; 18.e5 Nd7; 19.Re1 Bxe5; 20.Kf2 Bf6; 21.Re3 Nc5; 22.Rae1 Kd7. Black's pieces are much more active and the bishop pair is a tangible asset. Now White self-destructs, tempted by a sacrificial line, which is too easily declined. 23.Nxb5? f4!; 24.Re5 (24.R3e2 Nxd3+; 25.cxd3 cxb5.). 24...Nxd3+; 25.cxd3 cxb5; 26.Rxb5 Rb8; 27.Ne5+ Kd6; 28.Rxa5 Bh4+. White resigned.

7...exd4! A big theoretical novelty from Ligterink! After the game, Tal asked me why I chose the line, and was I familiar with his game against Alburt? I told him I was, but had an interesting idea in mind, but this move stopped me cold.

7...Qa5 was the old move, and here I was ready to employ an obscure idea. 8.Bxf6! Nxf6; 9.Nxe5 Nxe4; 10.Qf3! as in J. Brown vs. King, London 1978. But Ligterink's improvement at move 7 makes this moot.

Why didn't I consider the capture at d4? It is an obvious move. The answer is the lesson to be learned from this game. I had come across the Brown-King reference in a note in a book on the Veresov by Jimmy Adams. I knew that few people would be aware of it as Black (the game is still not in any databases, a warning to those who don't bother to consult good old fashioned books!) and was seduced by the chance to get a great game quickly.

This is poor thinking, especially since the players in the game were not professionals. Why shouldn't a strong experienced International Master like Ligterink play an inferior move and overlook a trap?

8.Nxd4. 8.Qxd4 was tried in the only other professional game I know of. Is it any accident my friend Joel Benjamin, who was also in the Reykjavik tournament (and went on to become a multiple U.S. champion), is playing Black? Well, my prepared line failed me, but delivered a point for him, 14 years later! 8...Qb6; 9.Qd2 Qxb2; 10.Rb1 Qa3; 11.e5 Nd5; 12.Nxd5 cxd5; 13.Bb5 Bc5; 14.Qxd5 0–0; 15.Bxd7 Bxd7; 16.Qxd7 Qxa2; 17.Qd1 h6; 18.Bh4 a5; 19.Ra1 Qb2; 20.Rb1 Qa2; 21.Ke2 g5; 22.Bf2 Rad8, Zhang Pengxiang vs. Benjamin, 2000.

8...Bb4.

Position after 8...Bb4

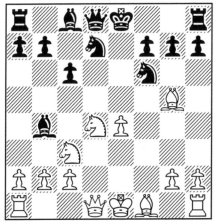

Black has at least equality, and I was psychologically devastated. I needed to find some active plan.

9.Nf5!? 0–0; 10.Bd3 Ne5; 11.Bxf6 Qxf6; 12.0–0. I wasn't fooled by the apparent attack. I know that to win on the kingside I need minor pieces. Watch them get swept off the board! **12... Bxf5!; 13.Rxf5 Qe7; 14.Qe2 Bxc3!** 14...Rad8 is also strong, but this move really clarifies the situation and leaves me with a terrible bishop and weak c-pawn.

15.bxc3 Qc5+; 16.Kh1 Qxc3; 17.Rb1 b5; 18.Rbf1 Rad8; 19.Qf2 Rd7.

Position after 19...Rd7

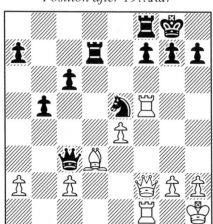

20.h3?! Up to now I have been playing the best moves, more or less. This move is very weak, though it doesn't appear to have any serious consequences in the near term.

20.Rh5 Nxd3; 21.Qf5!? might have been tried, but it isn't sound. 21...Nf2+!!; 22.Kg1 (22.Qxf2 Rd2; 22.Rxf2 g6; 23.Qxd7 Qe1+; 24.Rf1 Qxf1#). 22...g6!; 23.Qxd7 Nxe4!!; 24.Qd3! But not 24.Rh3 Qxd3; 25.cxd3 gxh5; 26.dxe4. (24. Rh3 Qc5+!; 25.Kh1 Nf2+; 26.Rxf2 Qxf2 and Black will win). 24...White is still busted and Black would have had to find some good moves. I never saw the idea at the board. Tal asked me about the move afterwards.

20.h4 Nxd3; 21.cxd3 Qxd3, with a tremendous game for Black.

20.Rg5!? h6; 21.Rg3 Nxd3; 22.cxd3 Rxd3 and Black has a great game.

20...Nxd3; 21.cxd3 Qxd3; 22.e5. The last chance. If I get the pawn to e6 I may have a small chance to survive.

22...Qc4. Nothing doing. **23.Rg5 g6; 24.Kh2 Re8; 25.h4? h6!** The game is lost. I set up a kamikaze attack on g6, but it is easily refuted. **26.Qf5 Qxh4+; 27.Kg1 Qd4+.** Black would capture the rook at g5 on the next move, so I gave up.

I was under a lot of pressure in preparation because if I won, a qualifying result for the title of International Master was almost certain. In addition, as the lowest ranked player in the 74-man field (I was going to be an arbiter, but rather than have an odd number of players, the organizers invited me to play) I was en route to a 6-5 result, ahead of a number of Grandmasters. This loss was avenged in the next round to earn my plus score and a respectable FIDE rating of 2370. Still, had I not been seduced by the possibility of a quick win, I might have done even better.

The game provides a second lesson, which is that when things go wrong, even boring equality is better than self-destruction! If I had more faith in my endgame play at the time (which would have been totally unjustified), I might have realized that you can win the game later, from an even position. Indeed, you have to do that much of the time as Black, first equalizing, and then playing for the advantage.

GAME LESSON FIFTEEN

If you find a good new move when preparing an opening, backtrack to consider options for your opponent, who may well have discovered "your" new move first!

GARBAGE STINKS!

Junk openings can be a lot of fun, and can be a part of a repertoire for blitz games, but they have no business in serious tournaments! The element of surprise is vastly overrated. You should be happy when your opponent plays an inferior move, even if it is new to you!

Now I'm not suggesting that all "unorthodox" openings are bad. Far from it! I wrote a very big book on the subject and found many interesting ideas. They must be used appropriately, however. More importantly, they must be judged objectively, without adding bonus points for surprise value unless there are complicated tactics involved.

The next game comes from a round-robin event in which I had plenty of time to prepare. My opponent, the late FM Eugene Martinovsky, was a friend. We had met frequently at the board, with the advantage heavily in his favor. He was a classical player, who would react predictably to the unusual, but still classical, Tayler Opening.

The move 3.Be2 is unambitious, but Michael Basman, the English International Master, who advocates many unusual openings, had been promoting a new gambit after 3...Nf6. A gambit approach seemed appropriate, and I later had more success with a different one. Since there was so little material on the opening, I just read what Basman had to say and didn't look too closely. Big mistake. The stench of White's position after ten moves could be detected anywhere in the room.

1.e4 e5; 2.Nf3 Nc6; 3.Be2 Nf6; 4.d4!? exd4; 5.e5 Ng4; 6.0–0 Ngxe5; 7.Nxe5 Nxe5; 8.Qxd4.

Position after 8.Qxd4

Schiller vs. Martinovsky, Illinois Tournament of Champions, 1986

Following Basman's opening recommendation, I felt confident I could get enough for the pawn after the retreat of the knight. But Black came up with a very interesting defense. **8...Qf6!** Nasty threat of ...Nf3+, winning the queen. **9.Qe4 Be7.** White's hope for an attack on the e-file against the enemy king is dashed. The king can escape to the kingside at any time. In fact, he just sits there and taunts me for the next ten moves! **10.Nc3 c6; 11.f4 Ng6; 12.f5 d5!; 13.Qa4 Bc5+!; 14.Kh1 Ne7.** Very effective reorganization by the veteran master. **15.g4 b5; 16.Qf4 h5!; 17.g5 Qxf5; 18.Qg3.** Two pawns down here, no trading queens! **18...Qe6.** 18...h4 was also good. **19.Bd3 0–0; 20.Bd2 Qg4?!; 21.Qe5 Qe6; 22.Qxe6?.** 22.Qg3 had to be played. I have no idea why I didn't keep the queens on, it could hardly be worse.

22...Bxe6; 23.Ne2 a6; 24.Ng3 g6. Black had little difficulty winning, though it took him a while.

GAME LESSON SIXTEEN
Avoid unsound openings in serious games!

DON'T IMPROVISE YOUR WAY INTO OPENING TRAPS!

Creativity and improvisation are important chess skills, but when playing a game, they are not generally applicable in the opening. During preparation at home, you can let your inspiration flow. At the board, stick to prepared move orders. The tempting new move you see at the board may well walk you straight into a trap!

1.e4 e5; 2.Nf3 d6; 3.Bc4 Be7; 4.d4 Nd7??. This is a well-known opening trap. In my desire to set up the Lion Formation, I casually switched the move order around. The price was very, very high.

5.dxe5! Nxe5; 6.Nxe5 dxe5; 7.Qh5 g6; 8.Qxe5.

Well, I'm down a pawn. My rook is attacked. My bishop is pinned. White has a huge advantage. What can I do? Resign? No, it is too early.

8...Nf6; 9.Bh6! Rg8; 10.Nc3.

Position after 10.Nc3

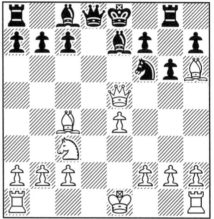

Baudo Mercere vs. Schiller, New York Open, 1998

Lesson one is over. Don't fall for opening traps! Now it is time for lesson two: Don't give up! Sure, Black's position would make a mother cry. The gods are laughing. At the prestigious New York Open my colleagues are trying not to laugh out loud. People stroll by the board and just shake their heads. It is very tempting to just concede the game and get out of the room.

10...Ng4!? I realized this wouldn't work, but my opponent, an experienced and literate Candidate Master who exploited my move order, was now under that typical pressure you feel when you have a game you know you should win.

11.Qf4 Nxh6; 12.Qxh6?! 12.Rd1! would have completely refuted my plan. However, White saw no reason to refrain from capturing at h6 and h7, with mate threat at f7.

12...Bg5!; 13.Qxh7 Qd2+!; 14.Kf1 Rf8.

Position after 14...Rf8

It must be admitted that Black has nothing for the pawns, really. Yet White must play accurately. It is logical to batten down the hatches and protect the pawns on the second rank. After all, if Black eats both the c-pawn and b-pawn then the game could get interesting.

However, passivity is rarely a good idea, Crawling into a shell concedes the initiative and gives the opponent time to act. White should have chosen a pawn sacrifice instead of defense. 15.Rd1! Qxc2; 16.Qg7 Qxb2; 17.Qe5+ Be7; 18.Qxc7! Black cannot take the knight because White will play Bxf7+ with discovered check, winning the queen.

15.Bb3?! Be6!?

I knew I'd need a lot of luck to win this game, but saw some tactical possibilities if only I could open the f-file. So I invited my opponent to do so, giving up a pawn and placing my king in mortal danger. I realized that I was doomed if my opponent finally got the rook to d1, but having spurned all previous opportunities, I suspected that White would pass on the move one more time. Bluffing doesn't work as well in chess as in poker, but when you hold a hand as bad as this, it is bluff or fold. Nothing to be gained by folding, and no way to raise the stakes. My opponent falls for it. He should have played

16.Rd1 Qf4; 17.Bxe6 where 17...Rd8!? (17...fxe6; 18.Qd7#); 18.Nd5 would have encouraged my immediate resignation. **16.Bxe6? 16...fxe6; 17.Qxg6+ Ke7; 18.Nd1.** White chooses an obvious defense of f2 over the weakening move 18.f3, but it was the wrong choice.

Position after 18.Nd1

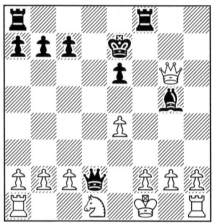

18...Rxf2+!! My turn now! I was still furious with myself for the opening play, but after this move I was all business again. I knew that I was close to equalizing, rebounding from a totally lost position. Those who strolled past my board thinking I was a complete idiot would see a miraculous escape! Perhaps even enough to redeem my earlier stupidity.

19.Nxf2 Rf8; 20.Qg7+ Rf7.

Position after 20...Rf7

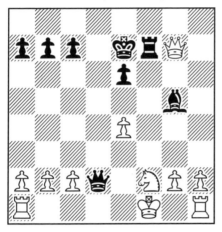

White has to give up the queen. On the other hand, with two rooks and two pawns for the queen, White is still way ahead in material. For the moment! My queen has been busy and she is hungry. Three queenside pawns make a tasty snack!

21.Qxf7+ Kxf7; 22.g3 Qxc2; 23.Kg2 Qxb2; 24.Rab1 Qxa2.

Position after 24...Qxa2

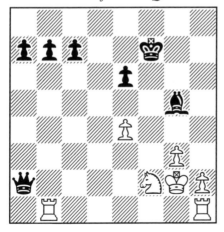

White can take the b-pawn, or go after the a-pawn. If you recall the first few tactical examples, you'll already suspect that a rook at a7 and a knight at e3 could run into trouble. Taking the b-pawn was correct. **25.Ra1? Qc2; 26.Rxa7?? Be3.** My opponent resigned, since I win the rook or the knight. I had been to the brink of the abyss, and with perseverance and a bit of luck, come away with a full point, to the astonishment of anyone who had passed by the board during the opening.

Does this mean you can get away whenever you fall for a trap? Hardly. Amazingly, I stumbled into a related trap a year later, and lasted all of 15 moves before toppling my king, and half of those were just available because my opponent made some inferior moves.

GAME LESSON SEVENTEEN

Stick to the move orders you know, because behind every transposition there may lie a trap!

DON'T BREAK TOO SOON!

One of the keys to playing effectively as Black is knowing the "breaks." These are pawn moves that challenge enemy pawns in the center. In Open Games (1.e4 e5), both ...d5 and ...f5 are available breaks. In the Sicilian, ...d5 is the right way to confront the e-pawn. In a Closed Game (1.d4 d5), both ...c5 and ...e5 are both available. A central break (...d5 or ...e5) is often the moves that levels the game and earns Black the cherished equality.

Knowing your breaks is part of standard opening strategy. Timing the breaks, that's another matter entirely. Usually a break has some small element of risk, as it opens up the position. Whenever a break is possible it should be considered, but you have to look at the downside, too. A typical break may work most of the time, but when it fails, it often fails spectacularly!

That's what happens in the next game. I rely on general considerations without doing the hard work of calculating concrete variations beyond a couple of moves.

1.e4 c5; 2.Nf3 e6; 3.d4 cxd4; 4.Nxd4 a6; 5.c4 Nf6; 6.Nc3 Bb4; 7.f3 d5? Well, I certainly knew that in the Sicilian you should play ...d5 as soon as it works, and that f3 often encourages it. But I underestimated the check at a4. **8.Qa4+ Nc6.**

Forced, as the bishop is attacked. It was easy enough to calculate through move 12, but I stopped there, satisfied that the symmetrical pawn structure was solid enough. **9.Nxc6 Bxc3+; 10.bxc3 bxc6; 11.cxd5 exd5; 12.exd5 Qxd5.** End of forced variation. **13.Ba3!**

Position after 13. Ba3!

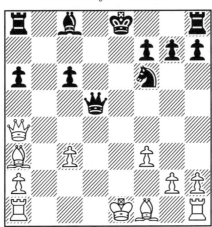

Reynolds vs. Schiller, University of Chicago, 1975

What a mess! Black cannot castle unless ...c5 can be played to block the bishop. The pin on the c-pawn is excruciating, but White threatens Bc4 and then after the king moves I am in trouble on the e-file. White can take the d-file at will with Rd1. So White owns all the open lines, and I've got ... nothing. **13... Bd7.**

The most important aspect of this move is that it prepares a discovered attack against the enemy queen. Although it is of no particular use at present, it can be a big asset later. In this game, it allows me to escape certain death! I didn't like the looks of

13...Qe5+; 14.Kf2 Qxc3; 15.Rd1! White can use the d-file for both attack and defense, while saving the e-file for the other rook. 15...Bf5 gets queens off. 16.Bc4! Qc2+; 17.Qxc2 Bxc2; 18.Rhe1+ Black has to give two pieces for the rook. 18...Ne4+; 19.Rxe4+ Bxe4; 20.fxe4. White wins easily, with two potent bishops and control of the d-file.

14.Bc4 Qe5+; 15.Kf2. Now Black seems to be in big trouble on the e-file, but a surprising tactic secures a draw. **15... Ng4+!; 16.fxg4 Qf4+.**

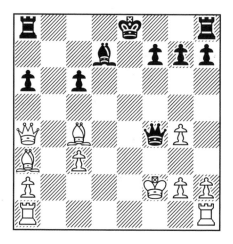

I offered a draw and my opponent accepted. Up to you to decide if he was wise... White could try to run to the queenside, but shelter is hard to find. If Black has time for ...c5 and kingside castling, White's king is in trouble. If 17.Kg1 Qe3+; 18.Kf1 Qf4+, a draw by repetition is coming. On the other hand 17.Ke1 Qe4+; 18.Kd2 Qxg2+; 19.Be2 c5!; 20.Qa5 Bb5 is messy. Not only is the bishop at e2 threatened, but also Black has time to castle. White was wise to settle for the draw!

GAME LESSON EIGHTEEN
Don't play the ...d5 break until you castle, unless you are absolutely sure it is safe.

♟ STEP FOUR
LESSONS IN THE MIDDLE GAME

While the opening and the endgame can be played with the help of positions studied in advance, the middlegame is, by definition, the area of the game where you need strategic thinking and pure calculation. General principles have to be used in place of prepared moves. The middlegame requires working out a plan and executing it precisely, which means getting the right moves in the right order. That's the first lesson in this chapter.

The demand for precision does not end after one move. In the next pair of lessons you will see how an excellent strategy can be ruined when a little slip takes place just when the goal is in sight. The following group of lessons is a variation on the same theme, but we deal with a very specific psychological error, when a player tries to be a bit too clever. Then we'll have a reminder about materialism and how it can lead you astray in a promising position.

When you have a disadvantage, there are techniques you can use to distract your opponent.

No, spilling coffee on the board isn't an option especially with the new regulations limiting caffeine at the board!

You can only use chess moves to distract your opponent, everything else is bad form, and usually against the rules. Fortunately, you can make moves that have a psychological effect of confusing your opponent, a technique which strong players use frequently, especially against lower rated opposition. Such "confusionary riffs," as they are called, are the topic of a pair of lessons.

Sticking to a defensive theme, we move on to a situation where survival is made more difficult when pressure is maintained for a long time. When you have forces in flexible positions, it is often possible to chase enemy units constantly, so that the opponent, even with more pieces or an attacking formation, has no time to take the initiative. During this campaign, the defending side is under great stress and is very likely to make a mistake.

The last lessons in this chapter cover a variety of situations that lend themselves to incorrect play for psychological reasons. Most sacrifices take place on squares occupied by an enemy piece. It often comes as a surprise when the opponent sacrifices a piece by moving it to an empty square right next to an enemy piece that can capture it.

One critical game lesson makes the very important point that while you should scrutinize the enemy positions for weaknesses that you can exploit, it is equally important to look in the mirror and see if your own vulnerabilities can be exploited. We close the chapter with a case of "nervous moves," where the mere possibility of earning a draw by repeating the position, when you know your opponent isn't interested in splitting the point, proves fatal.

BAD TIMING

It is important not only to find the right moves, but also to play them in the correct order. Often when two different move orders can reach the same position, a certain laziness sets in. It doesn't seem to matter which order is chosen, and in many cases that is indeed the case. But sometimes the move order is critical, as I found out in the following game.

Position after 22.Bd5

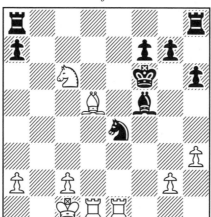

Pruess vs. Schiller, Mechanic's Masters
San Francisco 1998

22...Rac8?? 22...Nc3!; 23.Rd2 Rac8 was the correct move order, and Black would still be in the game. **23.Ne7 Be6.** 23...Kxe7; 24.Bxe4 Be6! I missed this resource, thought I'd have to exchange bishops with a bad endgame. After 25.Bd5 Rhd8! Black has nothing to worry about.
24.Nxc8 Bxd5; 25.Rxd5 Nc3; 26.Rc5 Rd8; 27.Rf1+ Ke6; 28.Nxa7 Nxa2+; 29.Kb2 and White won.

GAME LESSON NINETEEN
If you think that it makes no difference which of two move orders are used, think again!

LACKING THE FINISHING TOUCH - A

Unfortunately, I can provide a number of examples of games where I overlooked a winning plan in the final position. I've confined myself to two of the most painful. In each I take a draw by repetition when I could have simply finished off my opponent. Once the drawing line entered my mind, I mentally wrapped the game up with a half-point and simply didn't consider the possibility that I could actually win the game.

In the first example, this was rather typical of the games in the Tranmer Memorial, which was the first tournament with International Master qualifying norms to feature half men and half women in the ten player field. It was a very sociable event, as were all of the Brighton Internationals.

This was a fun event, even if many of the players seemed to suffer from lack of sleep. Perhaps it is unsurprising that several positions from that event appear in this collection. **1.e4 e6; 2.d4 d5; 3.Nc3 Bb4; 4.Bd2 dxe4; 5.Qg4 Nf6; 6.Qxg7 Rg8; 7.Qh6 Qxd4; 8.0–0–0 Bf8.** This is the most recommended defense for Black. **9.Qh4 Rg4; 10.Qh3 Qxf2; 11.Be3 Qf5; 12.Be2 Rg6; 13.g4 Qe5; 14.Bd4 Qg5+.** Black is well advised to accept the well-known draw with 14...Qf4+; 15.Be3 Qe5; 16.Bd4. **15.Be3 Qa5; 16.g5 Rxg5; 17.Qh4 Rg6; 18.Nh3 Bd6!?**

Position after 18...Bd6!?

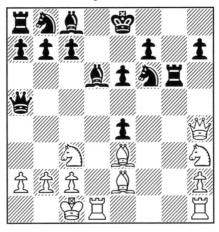

Schiller vs. N. Thomas, Eileen Tranmer Memorial
Brighton, 1985

A theoretical novelty. 18...Be7; 19.Nf4 and 18...Nbd7; 19.Nf4 are known to give White a strong attack. **19.Rhf1 Be5; 20.Nf4.** Not 20.Bh5, which allows the brilliant reply 20... Bg3!! **20...Bxc3!** Not 20...Nbd7, which allows White to win 21.Nxg6. **21.bxc3.** If 21.Nxg6 Bxb2+; 22.Kxb2 Qb4+. White may retain a small edge. **21...Nd5!** Black seals the d5. Or does he?

Position after 21...Nd5

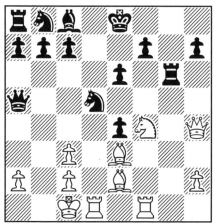

22.Rxd5! exd5; 23.Nxg6 Qa3+!; 24.Kd2 hxg6. So far so good, and I'm on my way to a brilliant win. But I stumble and fall. **25.Qh8+??** I missed the terminal 25.Rxf7!!, winning. 25...Qf8; 26.Qe5+ Qe7; 27.Qh8+ Qf8; 28.Qe5+. Instead, we agreed a draw.

GAME LESSON TWENTY

Even if you have used up most of your energy developing an attack, work as hard at the end as you did at the beginning!

LACKING THE FINISHING TOUCH - B

The second game featured a more common psychological error. I had been fighting from a terrible position all game. For some reason, this particular opponent often brings out the blunderer in me. In this case, an unsound sacrifice had rattled me and I lost my concentration. In flailing about, trying to survive, a draw by repetition was high on my list of goals. I took it, rather than the simple win.

Position after 16...dxe6

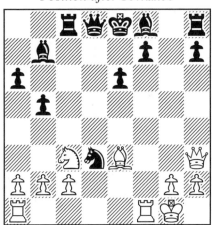

Blohm vs. Schiller, Frisco Masters, San Francisco, 2000

17.Rxf7!?; 17.Rad1 Rxc3!; 18.bxc3 Rg8 was what I expected. **17...Kxf7; 18.Qh5+ Ke7; 19.Bg5+ Kd7; 20.Bxd8.** I had already worked out my response, leading to a draw. **20... Bc5+; 21.Kh1.**

Position after 21.Kh1

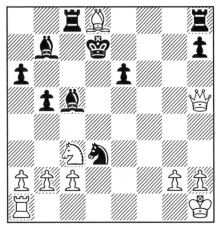

I was running scared, and was happy to escape with a draw by repetition. I didn't even look at the obvious winning line. **21...Nf2+?** 21...Bxg2+!!; 22.Kxg2 Nf4+ wins easily. **22.Kg1 Nd3+; 23.Kh1.** Draw agreed.

GAME LESSON TWENTY-ONE

Even when you are just trying to escape, be on the lookout for chances to win!

TOO CLEVER BY HALF - A

The next three examples show this opposite side of the coin. Instead of missing winning continuations and settling for a draw, I try to achieve much more than can be justified by the position. This kind of error is quite common among scholastic players. My students often tell me they played a move hoping for a specific line, and when the opponent sees what's up, the plan fails.

Position after 16.0-0

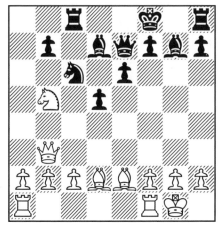

Bokan vs. Schiller, CNE Open, Toronto, 1971

16...Bd4? The error here is in trying to set up some cheap tactics, hoping White will run into a fork. If 17.Nxd4 Nxd4; 18.Qd3 Nxe2+; 19.Qxe2, I still can't play 19...Rxc2 because of 20.Bh6+! Instead, I wind up losing to a discovered attack. Better was 16...Rg8, though Black's position is in any case inferior. **17.Rad1.**

This sets up potential discovered attacks against my wayward bishop. **17...Rg8??** The bishop had to retreat; it is vulnerable at d4. **18.Nxd4 Nxd4; 19.Bh6+ Ke8; 20.Rxd4.**

Black is just a piece down. **20...Qf6; 21.Be3 e5; 22.Rxd5 Bc6; 23.Bb5 Qf3; 24.Bxc6+ bxc6; 25.Rxe5+.** I resigned.

GAME LESSON TWENTY-TWO

Avoid cheap tactics! Just because your opponent has already made a mistake doesn't mean that another one is likely.

TOO CLEVER BY HALF - B

Position after 25...Nf6

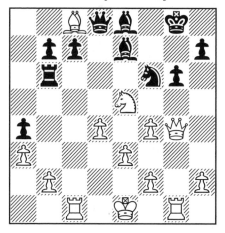

Schiller vs. Coull, Eileen Tranmer Memorial,
Brighton, 1985

I have a decisive material advantage, as long as I hang on to my bishop. I couldn't find a way to do that, even though it was fairly simple. **26.Qe2?** A tactical miscalculation. I thought this was very clever, threatening to check at c4 and grab her c-pawn. My piece on the 7th rank would attack the bishop at e7. This much I saw, but I missed a tactical nuance in this line, and one in the alternatives.
26.Be6+ Kg7; 27.Qf5! was what I missed. I failed to take into account the rook on g1, which preserves the pin on the g-pawn. 27...Rxb2; 28.Qd3 c5!?; 29.dxc5 Qa5+; 30.Kf1 Bxc5; 31.Rg5! and White wins. I considered only 27.Qh3 Rxb2; 28.Nd3 Rb6; 29.Ba2?
I couldn't see any deeper than this. (29.f5 Bxa3; 30.fxg6 hxg6; 31.Ra1 Qe7 was just too complicated.) 29...Bxa3; 30.Rc3 Qe7 is still very messy. **26...Qxc8; 27.Qc4+ Kf8; 28.Rc2.** 28.Qxc7 Qxc7; 29.Rxc7 Rxb2 is clearly better for Black.

Position after 28.Rc2

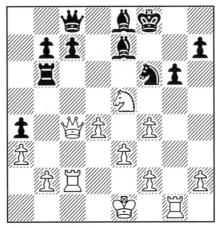

The game has become unpleasant. I'm not sure White is objectively worse, but Black's bishops will be stronger than White's rook.

28...Bd6; 29.f3 Rb3; 30.Qe2? This move gets me into trouble again! 30.Re2 b5; 31.Qc2 was a better defense, though Black has the initiative and can advance the b-pawn, which I dare not capture.

30...Nd5!

Position after 30...Nd5!

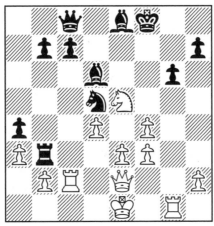

The game has swung completely in Black's favor. She can bring either the bishop or pawn to b5 in the near future. I should have retreated the knight to c4, but didn't want to abandon the outpost when I was certain the knight was immune from capture.
31.Qf2. 31.Nc4 Qe6 or 31.Ng4 h5 would not have been any better. **31...Rxe3+; 32.Kd1.** 32.Kf1 loses to Qh3+.
32...Qf5; 33.Rg4 Bxe5; 34.dxe5 Qd3+; 35.Kc1 Rxf3 and I gave up after a few more moves.

GAME LESSON TWENTY-THREE

Don't get so wrapped up in one line that you neglect resources available elsewhere.

TOO CLEVER BY HALF - C

Position after 17...Nf5

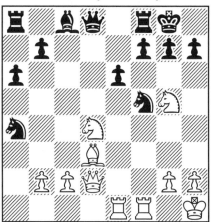

Schiller vs. Frenklakh, CalChess Championship, Foster City, 1996

ERIC SCHILLER • CARDOZA PUBLISHING

The game started out as a gambit. I have some compensation for the pawns, and should just capture at f5 with the knight followed by Qf4 with a direct attack on the pawn at f5 and the Black knight at a5 in direct line with my queen.

Instead, I decided to support d4 and open c2 for my queen, just to set up tactical tricks against h7 and a4. **18.c3?** After 18.Nxf5 exf5; 19.Qf4 Black can capture another pawn with 19...Nxb2, but after 20.Bxf5 Bxf5; 21.Qxf5 g6; 22.Qe5 the knight finds itself under attack.

GAME LESSON TWENTY-FOUR

If you have a choice between inflicting structural damage with an exchange or setting up tactical possibilities, the former is usually the better choice.

18...h6; 19.Ngf3 Nxd4; 20.cxd4 b5; 21.Bb1. Against a lesser opponent, White might be able to attack and achieve some compensation for the pawns, but Jennie was already too accomplished a player. Black eventually won.

GREED KILLS

Most players are careful enough to think twice about grabbing a pawn, especially against a strong player. When you can capture a pawn and protect one of your own, while attacking the enemy queen, the offer often seems too good to refuse.

Vigilance is always required, however, because even if there is no tactical trap, the pawn may nevertheless turn out to be poisoned. In the following example, the greedy capture turned out to be fatal.

Position after 25...fxe5

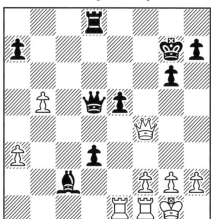

Schiller vs. Johansen, Four Nation Team Tournament, London, 1985

This is a tricky position. I had enjoyed a material advantage for most of the game, but had to worry about that d-pawn. I had just exchanged knights at e4. I can grab the e-pawn while protecting the rook, so why not? I didn't want to retreat the queen and lose the b-pawn, and had tactical qualms about 26.Qc1. **26.Rxe5?**

It wasn't hard to realize that 26.Qxe5+?? Qxe5; 27.Rxe5 d2 would lead to a good game for Black. 28.f3 d1Q; 29.Rxd1 Rxd1+; 30.Kf2 Kf6; 31.Rc5 Rd2+. I figured I'd be in deep trouble here, as the pawns don't make up for the bishop.

With 26.Qc1 I had to reckon with 26...d2! I'd have to give up the exchange and the b-pawn. 27.Qxc2 dxe1Q; 28.Rxe1 Qxb5 would have almost certainly led to a draw. The correct plan was the patient 26.Qd2! Qxb5; 27.Re4! The blockaders are in place and my other rook can enter the game, and then I can capture the f-pawn. Very good winning chances for White!

26...Qd6! A strong pin. **27.Rfe1. Or,** 27.Qe3 d2; 28.Qxa7+ Rd7; 29.Qe3 d1Q; 30.Rxd1 Qxd1+; 31.Qe1 Qxe1+; 32.Rxe1 Rb7 and Black wins. **27...Re8; 28.a4 d2.**

Position after 28...d2.

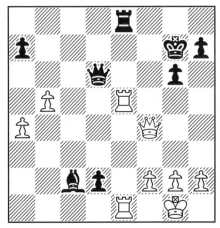

sI decide to sac the queen, probably the best White can hope for. **29.Qxd2!?** 29.Re7+ Rxe7; 30.Rxe7+ Qxe7; 31.Qxd2 Bxa4 is hopeless. **29...Qxd2; 30.Rxe8 Bxa4; 31.R8e7+ Kh6.** Without the queenside pawns, White has no real chances for survival.

GAME LESSON TWENTY-FIVE
A weak pawn need not be captured right away!

The rest of the game went **32.h4 Bxb5; 33.R1e3 a5; 34.Ra7 Bd7; 35.Re4 a4; 36.Re7 Qd1+; 37.Kh2 Qd4; 38.Ra5 Qxh4+; 39.Kg1 Qb4; 40.Ra7 Qb1+; 41.Kh2 Qb8+.** Time control reached. With no reason to play on, I resigned.

CONFUSIONARY RIFFS - A

When you have a bad position, it is often useful to play a confusing move, whether it is objectively good or not. The most successful "confusionary riffs" come about when you offer the opponent more than one capture on a single turn.

The opponent must often choose the proper capture or else lose the advantage. In the next game, I had a choice of captures, and I could have played both, had I done things in the right order.

Position after 34...Ne2

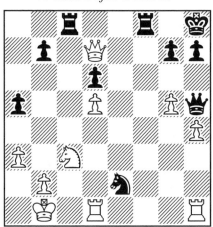

Schiller vs. Cramling, Gausdal International
Norway, 1984

White is clearly better, as long as the king remains safe. The Black d-pawn must fall. But it should not be eaten immediately! The clock was a factor here. White had nine minutes left, Black had just four. Black's last move presents me with a choice of captures. At first glance, they both seem reasonable.

After a couple of minutes deciding between Nxe2 and Qxd6, I chose greedily, and wrongly,

35.Qxd6? simplistically counting on the fact that after capturing on c3 with the knight, Black couldn't follow up with the rook because then the other rook at f8 would be undefended. The correct plan was 35.Nxe2 Qxe2; 36.Qxd6 with a solid advantage for White.

I played hastily, figuring I would need the precious few remaining minutes. That was an over-reaction, since only five more moves were needed, and one minute should be enough if your analysis is reasonably accurate. In any case, I devoted three minutes (1/3) of my time, but three minutes is just the average time per move in a professional tournament.

35...Rfd8? Cramling used half of her remaining time on this move, but missed a powerful shot. We both overlooked 35...Nxc3+!; 36.bxc3 Qe2! Although there is no immediate threat, White is actually lost. White can't allow a rook to get to f2, but there isn't much to be done about it. 37.Qe6 Qb5+!; 38.Ka1 Rce8. One rook will get to the seventh rank, and then it is game over.

36.Qb6! Saving the game. Although my king position is weak, I have just enough defense.

36...Nxc3+; 37.bxc3 Qf3!

Position after 37...bxc3!

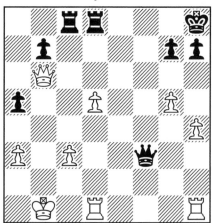

Just three moves to time control, which was the old, generous 40 moves in two and a half hours. With 6 minutes left I used up half my time, and again chose a bad move! With just two additional moves to make, I should have spent almost all of it, because the position is very complicated.

After playing this move, my next two moves would almost certainly have been part of analysis I had already carried out. **38.Qxa5?!** This is also a greedy move. I had to play. 38.d6 Qxc3; 39.d7 Rb8; 40.h5. White could keep playing to win, though the chances of a draw would be high.

GAME LESSON TWENTY-SIX

If two captures are the only reasonable moves, consider it a critical position and devote as much time as you need.

38...b6; 39.Qb4 Rxd5.

With 39...Rxc3, Black threatens ...Rb3+, but White was ready with a strong counter. 40.Rhf1! Rb3+. Forced, if the queen moves, there is trouble at f8. 41.Ka2 Rxb4; 42.Rxf3 Rxh4; 43.d6! A difficult game for Black, though not clearly winning for White.

40.Rdf1 Qd3+. Time control reached, with each player in their last minute.

41.Ka1 Rdc5; 42.Rd1. Draw agreed.

CONFUSIONARY RIFFS - B

In the next game, confusionary riffs explode all over the board, in many cases with each player having to consider multiple captures on consecutive moves. My opponent had rather recklessly sacrificed a piece at g4 and I had defended well obtaining a substantial advantage. On the last turn he advanced the d-pawn, creating a massive confusionary riff with a huge number of candidate moves.

In addition to possible captures at d4, I had to consider other moves such as retreating my knight to h2 to hit the queen, as well as an exchange sac at c6, which I could materially afford since I am up a piece for two pawns.

Position after 22...d4!?

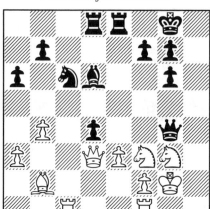

Schiller vs. Ivanov, Koltanowski Memorial
San Francisco, 2000

Offering up the pawn four different ways. I decide to take it with the queen, after getting rid of the pesky knight with an exchange sacrifice. **23.Rxc6?!** This was tempting, because Black's queenside pawns are so weak. But it is not correct.

23.exd4 Ne7 (or 23...Bxg3; 24.fxg3) 24.Rh1 Nd5!; 23.Nxd4 Bxg3; 24.fxg3 Ne5; 25.Qb3 Qe4+; 26.Kg1 Qg4 seemed a bit risky.

23.Bxd4! was best, in hindsight. I just didn't want the pin on the bishop, and my plan was to set up a battery with the queen ahead of the bishop, aiming at g7. I was a bit concerned about a possible ...Ne7-f5 plan. I also thought Black might get in ...Nxd4 and I'd have to recapture with the pawn, after which ...Bxg3 forces fxg3, and ...Re2+ would be available. I should have worked concretely on the line, which computer programs found easily.

23...Rxe3? Turnabout is fair play! My opponent also gets derailed thanks to the confusion of multiple captures. It is amusing that had he chosen the correct capture, I would have the burden of once again choosing between captures.

23...Bxg3! was the right plan. 24.Rxg6?! This was the prime candidate for me during the game. I don't know whether I would have played it if I actually had to analyze the position at the board. It would be yet another riff, with Black needing to choose the proper recapture. 24...fxg6; 25.Qc4+ Qe6; 26.Qxe6+ Rxe6; 27.Nxd4 Rxd4; 28.Bxd4 would have been fine for me, but 24...Qxg6; 25.Qxg6 fxg6; 26.Kxg3 dxe3; 27.fxe3 Rxe3 seems even. Instead, I would have been better off capturing with the pawn. 24.fxg3! sets up the next riff. 24...bxc6 would have to be played, though White is clearly better after 25.Nxd4. 24...Rxe3 runs into 25.Rxg6!! fxg6; 26.Qc4+, capturing the pawn at d4 after queens are exchanged at e6. If 25...Qxg6; 26.Qxg6 fxg6; 27.Nxd4 Black has 27...Rd3!; 28.Ne6 Rd2+; 29.Kh3 Re8 though with 30.Bc1! Rc2; 31.Nc5, White wins another pawn. **24.Qxd4 Qxf3+.** The theme continues! The alternative capture, or rather series of captures, is 24...Qxd4; 25.Nxd4 Rxg3+; 26.fxg3 bxc6; 27.Nxc6, but White will win. **25.Kg1 Bf8** or 25...Qf6; 26.Rxd6 Rxg3+; 27.fxg3 Qxd4+; 28.Rxd4 Rxd4; 29.Bxd4. **26.Qxd8!** Again the correct capture is necessary! 26.Qxe3 Qxe3; 27.fxe3 bxc6; 28.Bd4 Rd5. Black may be able to get rid of the remaining pawns. **26...bxc6.**

Position after 26...bxc6

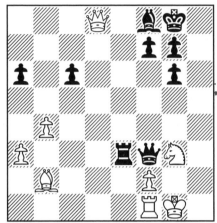

GAME LESSON TWENTY-SEVEN

When you have a bad position, look for moves, which give your opponent several ways to slip up, especially if the moves involve captures.

After all the complications of the past few moves, I was exhausted and saw a clean win, so I played it. I wasn't confused by the multiple captures here. I have to admit I never even considered the correct plan.

27.Qd4?! Good enough to win, but missing the shot! A much more appropriate tactical conclusion to the game could have been achieved with a surprising sacrifice. 27.Bxg7!! Kxg7; 28.Qd4+. Well, it could have been worse. I could have thrown away the win by choosing 27.fxe3?? Qxg3+; 28.Kh1 Qh3+ and Black draws.

27...Rd3; 28.Qe4 f5; 29.Qxf3 Rxf3; 30.Rc1 Rb3; 31.Rc2 a5; 32.bxa5 Bxa3; 33.Rc3! Black again has multiple captures, but neither one will save the game. **33...Rxb2.** 33...Rxc3; 34.Bxc3 Bc5 is refuted by 35.Ne2.

34.Rxa3 Kf7; 35.a6 Rb8; 36.Ne2 Ke7; 37.Nd4 Kd6; 38.a7 Ra8; 39.Ra6 Kc5; 40.Ne6+ Kb5; 41.Nc7+.
Black resigned.

SURVIVAL IS NOT A TEMPORARY OCCUPATION!

I've had plenty of experience fighting from bad positions, as many of the examples in this book show. In the next game I had gotten myself into a mess by stubbornly refusing to castle. Had things turned out differently, this would have been in the chapter on opening lessons.

However, my opponent let me off the hook and I swam and thrashed in muddy waters until a clear route to victory was in hand. Then I threw it all away. I was unable to make the adjustment between survival mode and simple defense. I sensed the source of the danger, but felt I could simply sidestep the problem by getting my king off the dangerous e-file.

After running for my life for a while, I felt a false sense of security, seeing only a single threat that I believed, falsely, was easily dealt with.

Position after 18.Nh3

Schiller vs. T. Taylor, New York City, 1979

After 18 moves I still haven't castled, and my king's knight has just made its first move. I'll get the king to safety next move, right?

18...Nc2+! Nope. I lose the exchange, and my king remains a target in the center.

19.Rxc2 Rb1+; 20.Ke2 Rxh1; 21.Nf2 Rg1; 22.g4 Qb4; 23.Kd3.

Position after 23.Kd2

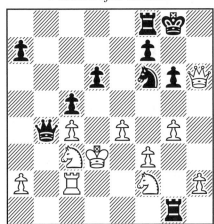

Hey, maybe I can hold on after all! The key squares are all protected.

23...d5!!

Wow, I didn't expect this clearance sac, which opens the e-file. After all, I have two pawns and a knight covering that square. **24.exd5 Nd7; 25.Nfe4?!** 25.Re2 was correct, anticipating trouble on the e-file.

25...Qb8? 25...Ne5+; 26.Ke3 f6 would have given Black a tremendous game.

26.Ng5! I knew that the situation was desperate, so I set up a checkmate, figuring he'd have to defend.

26...Ne5+; 27.Ke2 Re8.

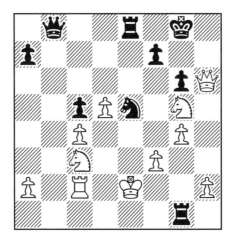

28.Kf2?? I didn't see Black's tremendous combination, which turns my win into a loss. 28.Nce4! would have put one in the win column. Perhaps I rejected the knight move because it was similar to the move that got me into trouble on move 25.

28...Nxg4+!!; 29.fxg4 Qf4+!!; 30.Kxg1 Re1+; 31.Kg2 Qxg4+; 32.Kf2 Qg1+; 33.Kf3 Qe3+. Faced with checkmate in three moves, I resigned.

> ### GAME LESSON TWENTY-EIGHT
> Even if you have weathered the first assault, make sure your king maintains plenty of protection at all times!

YES, YOU CAN SACRIFICE ON AN EMPTY SQUARE!

The battle was raging on both flanks. My first mistake was to press onwards with the attack, when I should have considered a defensive plan. Examples of that error can be found in the basic strategy lessons. The big mistake comes later in the game, when I failed to consider a sacrifice because no capture was involved. Sometimes a piece may move to a square to set up a simple fork or pin, but in trickier cases the goal is to deflect an enemy defensive piece. Most of the time these can be spotted when they are not buried in deep analysis. In the game, however, the move came as a shock even as it was played. I hadn't even considered the possibility!

The way to avoid such an error is to make sure you always take a look at the squares surrounding your king. Keep track of weaknesses in the position. If an enemy move stations a piece where it can hit a vulnerable point, make sure your defenses are sufficient. This is especially critical in positions with castling on opposite wings or when the king is stuck in the center.

Position after 16.Be2

Mont-Reynaud vs. Schiller, Falconer International
San Francisco, 1999

As usual, I got a little carried away and thought only of attack, when I should have first attended to defense.

16...Qh4? 16...Qa5! was much stronger. The queen can help defend the kingside and ...f5 is coming. White can try 17.f5 but 17...exf5; 18.exf5 Bd6 opens a path to the White king.

16...Rhg8+; 17.Kh1 Qg6 is a line I should have considered more carefully. I just assumed that 18.Rg1 would be good but in fact after 18...Qh7; 19.d5 Rxg1+; 20.Kxg1 Kb8. Black has a hidden defensive resource to bring the queen to a defensive position at e8 via ...Qg8+. For example, 21.dxc6 Nxc6; 22.Nb5 Qg8+; 23.Kh1 Qe8; and 24.Rxc6 fails to 24...Qxc6; 25.Qxa7+ Kc8, where White has no effective attack. **17.d5!; Kb8?!** 17...b6! would preserve Black's advantage, for example; 18.dxc6 Bc5; 19.Qf3 Nxc6; 20.e5 Nd4!; 21.Qa8+ Kd7; 22.Qxa7+ Ke8 and the king is safe at home on e8. The pawn at f4 is doomed. **18.dxc6 bxc6.** 18...Nxc6; 19.Nb5 Rd7! would have been my choice, had I seen what was coming. **19.Nb5!** This is the first sacrifice on an empty square, but not the last! **19...cxb5.** 19...Rd7! was the best defense, but I didn't see this idea until later. 20.Rfd1 Rhd8; 21.Rxd7 Rxd7 and the knight must retreat. The strong knight at b4 is probably enough to make up for the queenside weaknesses.

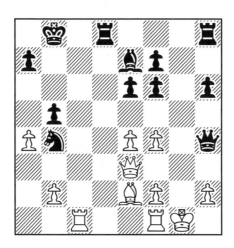

20.Rc7!! Ouch! If there had been a pawn at c7, I would have considered this possibility. The king cannot afford to leave the a-pawn unguarded, but the pawn is now under attack from both queen and rook. Nothing to do now, the game is lost. **20...Rhg8+.** 20...Kxc7; 21.Qxa7+ Kd6; 22.Rd1+ and mate is forced. **21.Kh1 Nc6; 22.Rxc6! Rd7!** 22...bxa4; 23.Rc7 would have been truly embarrassing! **23.Rfc1 Bd6; 24.e5.** 24.Qc3! would have been crushing. White is winning in any case.

GAME LESSON TWENTY-NINE

An empty square is just as valid a target as one occupied by an enemy piece!

24...fxe5; 25.Qc3 Qd8; 26.fxe5 Bc7; 27.Qb4! Qg5? Desperation. The threat of mate at g2 is serious, but White wins by striking first.
28.Qxb5+ Bb6; 29.Bf3 Rb7; 30.Qa6! With deadly threats! **30...Qe7.** 30...Bc7; 31.Rxc7 and mate in 6. Also terminal is 30...Qd8; 31.Rc8+ Qxc8; 32.Rxc8+ Kxc8; 33.Qxb7+.
31.R6c2 Bd4; 32.Qxb7+ Qxb7; 33.Bxb7 Kxb7; 34.Rc7+ Kb8; 35.Rxf7 Bxb2??; 36.Rb1. I resigned.

POSITIONAL WEAKNESSES UNDIAGNOSED

Position after 10.Nge2

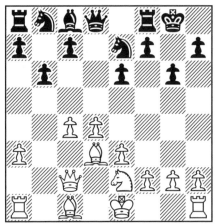

Giblen vs. Schiller, Under-1600 section
NYC Championship, 1970

Black's artificial opening play has created huge weaknesses on the kingside. The fianchetto position requires a bishop at g7, at least as long as White has a dark square bishop. While the long diagonal is closed, there isn't much danger. White can advance the d-pawn to open things up, but at least it will cost him a pawn. Rated in the 1500s at the time, I didn't appreciate such things, and played what must be, as far as strategy is concerned, one of the worst possible moves.

GAME LESSON THIRTY
When you have weaknesses, don't open up the position!

11...c5? This not only creates a serious weakness on the queenside, but more importantly opens up the h8-a1 diagonal. My kingside dark squares are too vulnerable for such an approach. If I had just placed my knight on d7 first, the plan would have worked. 11...Nd7; 12.0–0 c5; 13.dxc5 Nxc5; 14.Rd1 Nxd3; 15.Rxd3 Qc7 is completely equal.
12.dxc5 bxc5; 13.Bb2 Nbc6; 14.0–0 e5; 15.Rad1 Qc7; 16.Ng3 Rd8; 17.Ne4 Na5; 18.f4. White is threatening to open things up. **18...f5.** My weak dark squares are a terminal illness anyway. **19.Nf6+ Kf7; 20.Bxe5 Qc6; 21.Nxh7 Bb7; 22.Ng5+ Kg8; 23.Rf3 Rac8; 24.Rh3.** I resigned.

NERVOUS MOVES

When you are in an unfamiliar position at some stage of the opening, and a draw is an acceptable result, there is a temptation to try to get the queens off the board, assuming that the endgame holds no great risks. In some openings, including the Sicilian Defense, the nature of the game changes radically when the queens depart.

This is not a bad strategy, but when putting it into practice you have to keep in mind that unless the opponent is in a peaceable mood, the offer will likely be declined. The question you must ask yourself before maneuvering your queen into a position to exchange is how safe she will be.

In the following game, the team match circumstances were such that my job was to avoid a loss on first board, and let the rest of the team collect the points. I was a serious underdog against a highly skilled opponent. My nervousness was reflected in a bad decision to offer a trade of queens. As it turns out, the move was an error whether or not Black accepted! The position held great promise, actually, had I fearlessly pursued my kingside attack.

When playing under pressure, it is often best to shift the burden to your opponent by playing aggressively, even when you don't need to win. After all, if you have a strong attack, you are in a much better position to make your opponents draw offers they can't refuse!

Position after 14...O-O

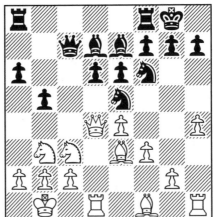

Schiller vs. Joshi, Pan American Intercollegiate Championship, Rhode Island, 1986

The game was played under a lot of pressure, as the University of Chicago team was relying on me to try to hold off the heavily favored Rhode Island team for the National Championship. Though my results in the tournament overall were excellent, I faltered here. My opening knowledge did not include this rare system with delayed castling. It was enough to take me out of my opening preparation. So I decided to try to swap queens, perhaps work against the pawn at d6, but mostly eliminate the danger of getting checkmated on the queenside. **15.Qb6?** 15.h5 Rfb8; 16.h6 was a bolder, and more correct approach. Nerves and lack of confidence after being outplayed in the opening deterred me. **15...Qc8!?** 15...Qxb6; 16.Bxb6 b4! would have been strong in any case. My whole plan was misguided. **16.Qd4 Rb8; 17.Bg5 Rd8; 18.f4 Nc6; 19.Qd3 Be8.** The game is swinging in Black's favor, with the ...d5 looming as a nasty threat, and ...b4 to worry about. **20.Re1.**

An interesting idea, to get some play on the e-file when ...d5 comes. **20...a5.** 20...b4 might have been played. 21.Nd5!? was, rightly or wrongly, my idea. 21...exd5; 22.exd5 with a messy position that probably is better for White. **21.Nd4?** 21.h5 h6; 22.Bh4 would have kept hopes of a kingside attack alive. **21...Nxd4; 22.Qxd4 b4; 23.Nd1 Qc7; 24.Ne3?!**

I was in a hurry to get this knight back into the game. 24.Bd3 would have been better, also defending c2 but aiming at h7. Perhaps something like Qe3-f3-h5 would be available later. **24...h6; 25.Bxf6.** There are no miracle sacrifices in this position. I spent some time searching in vain. **25...Bxf6; 26.Qc4 Qb6; 27.Ng4.**

Position after 27.Ng4

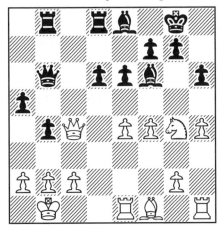

27...Bc3! I can't take the bishop without losing my queen. I'm really on the run now. **28.Rd1 h5; 29.Nh2 d5?** (29... Bc6 should have been played first.); **30.exd5 Rxd5; 31.Rxd5 exd5; 32.Qe2 Qd4; 33.Nf3 Qxf4; 34.Qd1 Bf6.** The position is hopeless. I played on another ten moves, but could not save the game.

35.Bd3 a4; 36.Qc1 Qc7; 37.Qe3 Bd7; 38.Ng5 Re8; 39.Qc1 a3; 40.Re1 g6; 41.Rf1 Qe5; 42.Nf3 Qxb2+; 43.Qxb2 Bxb2; 44.Ng5 Re7; 45.Rd1 Bg4. I resigned.

Although I lost the game, our team won the Pan American Intercollegiate title. I had played well in my other games, especially my Sicilian Dragon encounter with Herbst, which is still cited in many Dragon sources.

GAME LESSON THIRTY-ONE

If you want to offer your opponent a draw, it is best to do that with a draw offer, as playing for a repetition of moves can prove costly.

♟ STEP FIVE
Lessons in the Endgame

For many years, weak endgame play was often characteristic of American chess, and to some extent it still is. Avid tournament players will spend a lot of time, effort and money on opening preparation, but endgame study has rarely been a priority. There are a few sensible reasons for this.

Endgame study, especially if attempted alone, is not a lot of fun. In many ways, I was typical of my generation in studying openings obsessively, neglecting the less fascinating fundamentals. Working with a personal trainer is the most effective, and often most enjoyable, method of acquiring necessary endgame and middlegame skills. That involves a lot of commitment, and is uncommon in a country where chess is primarily played for fun.

Another difficulty presented by endgame study is its huge mass. There are hundreds of positions that simply must be known in order to play effectively. One reason that computers have had difficulty in mastering endgame play is the need to develop target positions and find ways to reach those goals.

That is quite different from a brute force search which is always limited at some point to a certain depth. Recently, programs have been developed which take advantage of encyclopaedic knowledge and databases of all possible positions featuring very few pieces. Human beings just don't have the capacity to process so much data.

In my case, serious endgame study didn't start until I was in my late twenties. I had a game against Grandmaster Tony Miles at the 1981 Regency Masters that forever changed my attitude.

Though I had lost many endgames through lack of knowledge, laziness prompted me to take the attitude that since there was so much I needed to know about the endgame, and so little that would apply in any one game, that I could rely primarily on calculation. The game with Miles was a brief adventure. I misplayed the opening, but came up with an ingenious way to obtain a nearly equal game. The cunning Grandmaster then tempted me to enter one of a variety of endgames. I recall that there were six different endgames available, four of which were quite drawable, one that could be held with precise play, and a horrible rook endgame with even material. Of course I chose the last one (rook endgames with even material should be drawn, right?) and went down to defeat quickly.

The memory of that game lasts as long as the more successful and entertaining effort in that event against Paolozzi, presented in the Lessons Learned chapter. I realized that I simply had to learn how to play endgames better. It took me some time, but I've managed to play quite a few excellent endgames and achieve some extra points, though I also still have unforgivable gaps in my knowledge, as you'll see in the following games.

Half of each lesson I give to my students is usually on the endgame. Applying methods I learned from Garry Kasparov's trainer Alexander Nikitin, I've been able to make endgame study both intellectually challenging and fun. I wish I had been able to learn endgames properly when I was young. It would have spared me a lot of grief! Even if you don't consider yourself a serious chessplayer, endgame study will lead to many more pleasurable experiences and it is worth the effort. When you understand the endgame you can choose wisely when you are faced with a decision on keeping the queens on the board.

The six lessons in this chapter don't even scratch the surface of necessary endgame knowledge. I've written several books on the endgame, but here I am concentrating on the psychological and preparation aspects of the endgame.

The fundamental king and pawn endgames and the concept of the opposition are familiar to most chessplayers, but many players stop there and don't bother to learn the dozens of crucial king and pawn endgames, which are tricky. These are best learned from endgame studies, which usually combine several important themes. Such positions are hard to play, if you don't know them, and it is easy to go wrong, as in Schiller vs. Mar.

Knowing the basics can actually hurt you if you place too much confidence in platitudes such as the "bishops of opposite color usually draw." It is never quite that simple, and it is important to try to analyze endgames deeply and not stop when some general consideration kicks in.

The endgame requires more objectivity than earlier phases of the game. In many cases, the "correct" result is already known, at least to computers and reference books. If the position is drawish there isn't too much that can be done about it. Excessive ambition can bring ruin, leaving the player with no points instead of the half-point a draw would have earned. Schiller vs. Ravikumar shows the danger.

In many endgames, a particular move is necessary and cannot be omitted, whether or not it seems relevant or best at the time. This mistake happens most frequently when long and elaborate calculations are being made. You can get so caught up in various long-term considerations that you forget about some basic move that must be played right away.

In Shamkovich vs. Schiller, we see how important it is to pay as much attention to empty squares as those that are occupied. In endgames, many of the squares are empty but may play a critical role if the enemy is allowed to take advantage of them.

KNOW ALL THE BASIC KING AND PAWN POSITIONS!

If you understand which pawn endgames are decisive and which are likely to be drawn, you can make good decisions on trading pieces. In the next game I handle that part of the decision process well. However, though I instinctively felt the position was drawn, I didn't remember how to do it! The drawing method is well known, but if it lies out there in books, it can't help you. It has to be burned into your memory.

Position after 38.g4

Grefe vs. Schiller, People's Open, Berkeley, 1994

With White short of time, and confidence in the pawn ending, I decided to be confrontational.

38...Na5+!? There is no need for this, and of course it is an irrevocable action. But I was confident I could draw the king and pawn endgame. My instincts were correct.

But "can" isn't the same as "does." After, 38...f5, the endgame should be drawn without too much trouble, but I wasn't sure. In any case, I knew that the former U.S. Champion would torture me until all time controls were exhausted. By the next year I had mastered the position with knight vs. bishop with this sort of pawn structure, as you'll see in the Lessons Learned chapter. **39.Bxa5 bxa5; 40.Kd4.** White holds the opposition. That's a big advantage in a king and pawn endgame. White also has the b4-break as an option. Black must defend rigorously. **40... h6?! 40...g5; 41.**Ke4 Ke6; 42.f5+ Kd6; 43.Kd4 Kc6; 44.Kc4 is the correct plan. **41.h4 Kc6; 42.Kc4 Kd6; 43.b4.** We both misjudged this move, though the alternative isn't better. 43.h5 gxh5; 44.gxh5 Kc6 (44...f5 allows 45.Kd4); 45.f5 Kd6 is a draw. **43...axb4; 44.Kxb4 Kc6; 45.Ka5 Kb7.** I think we both saw this position before the minor pieces came off. I thought this would draw easily. **46.g5 fxg5; 47.fxg5 hxg5; 48.hxg5 Ka7; 49.Kb4 Kb6; 50.a5+.**

Position after 50.a5+

50...Kc6?? A study-like draw was available, and I should have known it. The problem was I had been calculating too much, and either didn't know or didn't remember the drawing line. Of course I was also exhausted, but then you have to be prepared to play endgames even in two-game-a-day tournaments.

If I had recalled this basic endgame idea I would have truly earned my half-point. My instincts had held up, and I had reached the drawing line with my bold move ...Na5. All for naught, because I didn't know a simple drawing method! 50... Kb7!; 51.Kb3 Kb8!! does the trick.

51.Kc4.

Position after 51.Kc4.

The control of the opposition wins for White. I didn't resign yet, because it is my rule to resign only when the result is obvious even to very weak players. After all, I hate to be asked why I resigned, as if the position were drawn! I give this same advice to my students.

Don't play on to the point of being silly. Play the obvious moves at the end quickly, and use the few moments to compose yourself before a courteous resignation. Those who know me, know that sometimes takes more than a few seconds!

GAME LESSON THIRTY-TWO
Study your king and pawn endgames thoroughly!

51...Kd6; 52.Kd4 Ke6; 53.Kc5 Ke7; 54.Kb6 Kd6; 55.Kxa6 Kc6; 56.Ka7 Kc7; 57.a6. I resigned.

BISHOPS OF OPPOSITE COLORS DON'T ALWAYS DRAW

When bishops of opposite colors are on the board, it is much easier to hold a draw in an endgame where you are a pawn or two down. Sometimes even three pawns aren't enough to win. It is easy to be lulled into a sense of false security, especially when there are rooks on the board. Rooks and bishops work well together.

In the following game, my opponent has a dangerous passed pawn, and although I control the promotion square, I underestimated the unchallenged power of the Black bishop.

Position after 35...Bg5

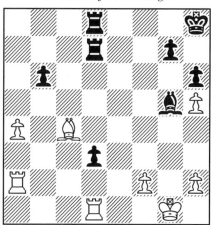

Schiller vs. Mar, Golden Bear Class Struggle
Berkeley, 1998

36.Ra3? 36.a5 was absolutely necessary to eliminate the pawn that eventually leads to White's defeat. 36...bxa5;

37.Rxa5 d2; 38.Re5 would not be fun for White, but some resistance was possible.

36...d2; 37.Kf1 Rc8; 38.Be2 Rc1; 39.Ra1 Kg8; 40.a5. Too late. **40...Rxa1; 41.Rxa1 Bf6!** I simply overlooked this powerful move. **42.Rb1 bxa5; 43.Bc4+ Kf8; 44.Ke2 Bc3; 45.Rb8+ Ke7; 46.Bb3.** Finally the bishop controls the promotion square. One move from salvation, but it is one move too many.

46...d1Q+!; 47.Bxd1 Rd2+. I resigned.

GAME LESSON THIRTY-THREE

Bishops of opposite color do not guarantee an endgame draw even when material is equal!

EXCESSIVE AMBITION

When playing with confidence, the ambitious variations are usually the most appealing. Often the best plan is to settle for a boring, drawish position. When paired against stronger opposition, playing for a draw risks being ground down in an endgame by superior technique. This can lead the lower rated player to try to bring the endgame to a boil by introducing complications, taking the game out of the realm of pure technique where the opponent has superior skills.

The problem with this way of thinking is that the higher ranked player is probably a superior tactician too. Somehow the notion takes root that every complicated position brings the chance that a lucky punch can score a knockout.

In the next game, the psychology wasn't quite like that. I was having a great tournament, and knew I was playing well. In the opening, I offered a gambit that my opponent declined, and the result was a very boring, symmetrical position. Instead of sitting on the position, I decided to go for an attack in the endgame. My gambit mood had continued into the endgame, where such subjective thinking really didn't have any place.

Patience was a lesson I had not yet learned, and it would be another decade before I began to appreciate the slow and steady positional approach.

Position after 18...Rd8

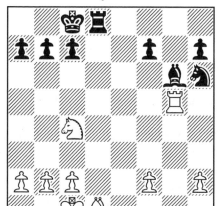

Schiller vs. Welin, Reykjavik Grand Open, Iceland, 1986

The opening had led to a drawish, symmetrical game. White has no reason to believe that active play is going to bring anything special. After a simple move, say 19.Ne3, it is hard to see anything but a draw resulting. I had been playing well in the tournament, and wasn't worried that my opponent was a strong International Master.

I figured he would play on for some time in any case rather than concede a draw to the lowest ranked player in the tournament. This makes my decision to play ambitiously highly suspect.

19.Ra5. Objectively, there is nothing wrong with this move. Instinctively, I felt that if Black went after the kingside pawns, as expected, I'd be able to use all three of my pieces against the enemy king, which had only a few pawns as guardians. I guess neither of us was in the mood for a draw.

It turns out that my instincts were correct, but I lacked the technique of, say, Mikahil Tal, to carry out the attack. I know this because Tal joined us after the game and rattled off a number of fascinating "fantasy variations" leading to wins in 20 moves or so! I wish I had been able to take notes on all of them, but we were too busy analyzing. That isn't to say the position was objectively winning, as the lines did need more than a bit of cooperation from my opponent, but I must confess I didn't even see the main ideas of his beautiful lines during the game.

19...Rd4; 20.Ne5. 20.Ne3 Rh4; 21.Rxa7 Kb8; 22.Ra5 Rxh2; 23.f4 Rf2; 24.Nd5 b6; 25.Ra4 is how some of the analysis started. The position eventually wound up with tricks on the a8-h1 diagonal, but all I remember is that somehow the Black rook wound up on h1 and White used Ra8+, ...Kxa8, and a bishop check on the long diagonal.

The position after 25.Ra4 is even, as White can play Rc4 to help defend c2. **20...Rf4; 21.Rxa7 Kb8; 22.Ra3 Rxf2; 23.Nd7+ Kc8; 24.Nc5.**

Position after 24.Nc5

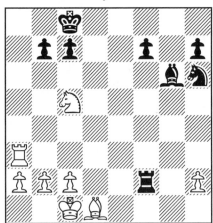

This was the position I was aiming for, threatening a back rank mate. The problem is the bishop at d1, which must remain in place to guard the pawn at c2, which cannot be sacrificed because the knight at c5 would fall to ...Rxc2+. So Bf3 is not in the near future.

There was, however, an interesting alternative in 24.Nf8!? I didn't consider this method of controlling d7 and attacking g6 at the same time. The bonus here is that Rh3 can lead to the win of the h-pawn. 24...Kd8; 25.Rh3 Nf5; 26.Nxh7 Nd4; 27.Ng5! Ne2+; 28.Bxe2 Rxe2; 29.Rc3 Rxh2; 30.Nf3 Rg2; 31.Ne5 should be drawable.

24...c6; 25.h4 Rh2; 26.Ra4? This is a very bad move. The rook is not designed for passive defense. As my endgame education progressed, I developed a greater respect for having an active rook, which is often enough compensation for a pawn.

If this were a pure rook endgame, I would have played a more active move, but with the minor pieces on the board I didn't want to let the h-pawn go.

26...Nf5; 27.Rb4 Ne3!

Position after 27...Ne3!

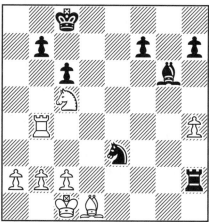

How ironic. It is the three Black pieces attacking my own king! I hadn't thought about that when I went after the queenside. I had only analyzed the capture of the h-pawn. On 27...Rxh4; 28.Rxb7 Rc4 I was going to play 29.Nb3, intending to fork at a5 if Black takes the rook.

I thought this very clever, but had the game gone this way it would have landed in the Too Clever by Half section. 29... Rxc2+!!; 30.Bxc2 Kxb7; 31.Nc5+ Kc7 is a terrible endgame for White.

28.Ne4. 28.Rd4 Bxc2; 29.Bg4+ Nxg4; 30.Rxg4 Bf5 was a miserable alternative. **28...c5; 29.Ra4 Kb8; 30.Nc3??** In time pressure, I drop the game with one move. I doubt I could have survived in any case, since the passed f-pawn will fly up the board. **30...Nxd1.** I resigned. If I capture with the knight, then ...Rxc2+ is deadly. If I use the king, then ...Bxc2+ wins the exchange.

GAME LESSON THIRTY-FOUR

In the endgame, maintain absolute objectivity at all times!

FORGETTING TO PLAY A NECESSARY MOVE

One error, which is always hard to explain, is forgetting to play a move. Sometimes after a long period of analysis, most of which assumed a starting move, you just forget what the move was supposed to be. In other cases, such as the next game, the explanation is somewhat different.

In this game, the natural move is rejected because it doesn't accomplish the obvious goal. However, it was needed for defensive purposes.

Position after 29...exd5

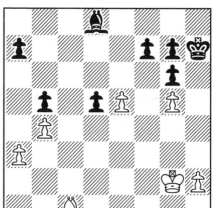

Schiller vs. Ravikumar, Four Nation Team Tournament,
London, 1985

How could I possibly lose this endgame as White? I have an inferior bishop, but the Black king can't infiltrate.

GAME LESSON THIRTY-FIVE

After thinking for a long time, review the initial position and check again for any threats or positional factors you might have overlooked.

I forgot to play 30.Be3 here and, as a result, my opponent's bishop transformed itself into a monster. I had realized that on Be3, I had no threat at a7 because my g-pawn would be undefended. So I figured I'd take care of that little problem before moving my bishop.

30.h4? Bb6! I will now have to wait until my king is in position before challenging the enemy bishop on the a7-g1 diagonal. Unfortunately this gave Black time to implement both defensive and offensive plans.

31.Kf3 Bd4; 32.Kf4 a6; 33.Be3 Bb2! My opponent's superior bishop will grab my weak pawns. **34.Bc5 Bc1+; 35.Be3 Bxa3; 36.e6 fxe6; 37.Ke5 Bxb4; 38.Kxe6 Bc3; 39.Kf7 d4.** There is no stopping this pawn now. The remainder of the game was just a matter of seeing if Black could make time control. **40.Bf4 d3; 41.h5 d2; 42.hxg6+ Kh8.** White resigned.

EYES FOR THE WRONG SQUARE

In the endgame, it is important to cover squares that can be used by your opponent to create problems. Often, it is quite obvious which squares qualify for special treatment, but some endgames, especially those involving knights, are much harder to diagnose.

In the next game, there are two potential critical squares, but one is more important than the other. I chose the wrong one.

Position after 65...Ke3

Schiller vs. Kosten, Four Nation Team Tournament London, 1985

I have managed to get to an endgame with a rather bad bishop against a strong knight. Surely it can be defended, since I don't have any undefended properties. There is only one real chance for Black, and that is to somehow contrive to play ...c5 and liberate the d-pawn. **66.Be7?** 66.Be5! is the move. I had to keep my eye on the c7-square. I didn't appreciate that, thinking only of c5. **66...Nc7!; 67.Bc5 Ke4.**

Position after 67...Ke4

It is now clear that Black plans ...Ne6 and then I can't avoid the ...c5 break. **68.Kd2 Ne6; 69.c3?** This hastens the inevitable. 69.Kc3 Nxc5; 70.dxc5 d4+; 71.Kc4 Ke3; 72.b4. Forced. 72...Kd2; 73.Kxd4 Kxc2; 74.Kc4 Kb2; 75.Kd4 Kb3 and Black wins.
69...Nxc5; 70.dxc5 d4; 71.c4 d3; 72.b4 Kd4; 73.b5 Kxc4; 74.bxa6 bxa6; 75.Kd1 Kxc5; 76.Kc1 Kd4; 77.Kd2 c5. White resigned.

GAME LESSON THIRTY-SIX

In the endgame, pay as much attention to empty squares as to occupied squares.

ADJOURNMENT ANALYSIS DEBUGGED AT THE BOARD

Before the computer chess age took hold, most tournament games were adjourned after four to six hours and then resumed the following morning. This provided excellent opportunities to deeply study endgame positions, with real rewards for hard work. At professional events, positions were not usually analyzed alone. A player would seek out friends among the competitors and take advantage of all available resources.

When the game was adjourned, there was the matter of selecting a sealed move to be placed in an envelope and revealed the next morning at the resumption of play. Once in the envelope, the move cannot be changed, so it was important to choose wisely.

The timing was important too. Often a player would hold back a move until the arbiter was approaching the table, and play it just in time so that the opponent would have to seal and wouldn't have the benefit of overnight analysis on the move.

The art of adjournment analysis, which generally was restricted to a few hours since sleep is also important, was a true test of endgame understanding. I learned a tremendous amount from these sessions, often getting the benefit of Grandmaster advice. In the next game, I would normally have turned to my friend and frequent co-author, Grandmaster Leonid Shamkovich, but he was my opponent!

My choice of sealed move was a reasonable one, but not best. That's not always a terrible thing, since the opponent is likely to spend most of the analysis time on the most important lines in the critical variations. I found myself on the receiving end when the game resumed. My opponent chose a line that wasn't as strong as the one we had concentrated on.

The game followed a branch of analysis that we hadn't considered critical, and I was caught by surprise. When an error in your preparation, whether in the opening or endgame, shows up at the board it is always a very uncomfortable experience.

If games were adjourned these days, powerful computer programs would be available to assist with analysis. The game would likely conclude with the best moves for each side leading to an inevitable conclusion. However, you should consider using adjourned games (or just selected endgame positions) as part of training. I use this exercise with advanced students.

Position after 44.Ke3

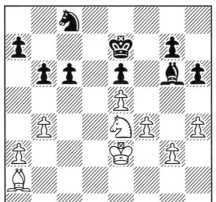

Shamkovich vs. Schiller, Gausdal International Norway, 1984

Unfortunately there was double pressure here. We were into the second time control and the arbiter would soon approach with the envelope into which I would have to place my sealed move. There are several possibilities.

I could try to hold the knight vs. bishop endgame after exchanging on d4. The Grandmaster had played the last few moves quickly, forcing me to think on my own. If the game were to be adjourned, I'd have a chance to analyze with Grandmaster Jansa, with whom I had already had many instructional endgame sessions as we both seemed headed for adjournments in almost every game.

I didn't want to commit myself to the capture on e4 until after adjournment. I sought out a waiting move, but couldn't find one. I then saw that by advancing the c-pawn, I could get to a forcing variation that would make the adjournment analysis much easier.

44...c5!? 44...Bxe4; 45.Kxe4 g6 was the alternative, with the likely continuation; 46.Bc4 b5; 47.Bd3 Nb6; 48.Kd4+-. 44...Kd7; 45.g4 Ne7; 46.Nd6 h5!; 47.gxh5 Bxh5. White's weakened pawn structure gives Black some chances. It isn't clear how White could make progress. This would have been the best plan, but I had a feeling that with a less forcing line my opponent would surely find a way to capitalize on his positional advantages.

45.bxc5 Bxe4; 46.Kxe4 bxc5.

Position after 46.Kxe4

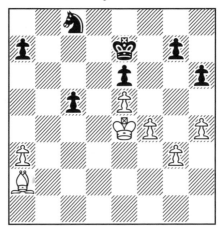

This much was predictable. Black has four pawn islands, and it is very difficult for the knight to defend. The passed c-pawn is just weak. White's strategy is clear: break through on the kingside.

47.g4. We expected 47.Kd3 Nb6; 48.h5. White should have prepared the kingside advance in this way, instead of plunging right in. In fact, the adjournment analysis concentrated on this line. **47...Nb6?!** This inferior move was chosen because of an error in analysis later on. My scoresheet shows I took only about ten minutes to play up to move 53, and only at move 54 was I taken out of the adjournment analysis. **47...g6!** would have been best. I can't recall why this move was rejected. I think it was mostly a matter of not wanting to put the pawn where the bishop could get at it. But that is lazy thinking. With the knight at b6, the formation is solid enough to draw.

In choosing between the move orders, I obviously (in hindsight) failed to evaluate the position at move 53 properly. **48.f5!** Critical, because otherwise I can repair the error with ...g6. **48...exf5+; 49.gxf5 Na4; 50.Bc4!** If 50.Kd3 Nb2+; 51.Kc2 Na4; 52.Kb3 Nb6, then the wall holds. **50...Nb6; 51.Bg8!**

Position after 51.Bg8!

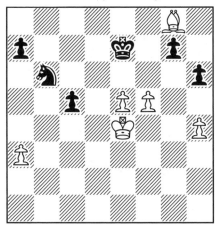

White finds the correct plan. The king will infiltrate via d5 after Black eventually runs out of moves.

51...Na4? Passive play is unpleasant. Being ground down by a Grandmaster is often even more unpleasant, as reprieves are rarely granted. I figured that I couldn't keep the king out forever, so might as well get it over with. Bad decision. The correct line was 51...Kd7; 52.h5 Ke7; 53.Be6 a5; 54.Ke3 Ke8; 55.f6. Otherwise there is no way to make progress. 55...gxf6; 56.exf6 Kf8; 57.Ke4. Black must give way. 57...a4; 58.Ke5 Ke8; 59.Kf5 Kf8; 60.Kg6 c4; 61.Kxh6 c3; 62.Bf5 Kf7; 63.Kg5 Nd7; 64.h6 Nxf6; 65.h7 Nxh7+; 66.Bxh7 Ke6; 67.Kf4 Kd5; 68.Ke3 Kc4; 69.Bc2.

White wins, because the bishop is of the correct color to support the a-pawn. Although this line is very long, it was easy to analyze. So during the analysis session, 51...Na4 had been prepared. However, no further time was spent on it. **52.Kd5 Kf8; 53.Bh7 Ke7; 54.Bg6.**

Position after 54.Bg6

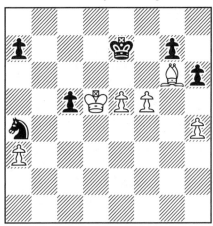

How is White to make progress? I wasn't quite sure. **54... a6; 55.Bh5 Kd7; 56.Bf3 Ke7; 57.Bg2.** Shamkovich just marks time while I run out of moves and drop the c-pawn. **57...a5; 58.Bh3 Nc3+; 59.Kxc5 Nb1.**

Position after 59...Nb1

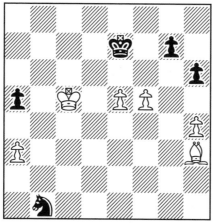

This was the type of defense I had come up with at the board. White can't defend the a-pawn. So with all the queenside pawns gone, I can bring the knight to the kingside, annoy the kingside pawns, and get a draw.

GAME LESSON THIRTY-SEVEN

Always double-check adjournment analys is at the board.

60.Bf1! I hadn't reckoned on this retreat! **61...Nd2.** Not 60...Nxa3? because of 61.Bd3! The knight cannot escape, and will be captured after Kb6xa5-a4. This was the tactic I missed. A simple domination theme in pure form!

61.Bd3 Nf3; 62.Kd5 a4 or 62...Nxh4; 63.Be4! with domination on the other side of the board! I couldn't miss this after my horrible realization at move 60! **63.h5 Nd2; 64.Be2 Nb3; 65.Bd1 Kf7** or 65...Kd7; 66.Kc4 Nd2+; 67.Kd3 Nb1; 68.Bxa4+ Ke7; 69.Bb5 Nxa3; 70.Ba6. Again the knight is trapped. **66.Kd6 Nd4; 67.e6+ Kf6; 68.Bc2!** I resigned.

There is no way to prevent White from getting a new queen. If 68...Nxc2; 69.e7 Kf7, then 70.Kd7 Nxa3; 71.e8Q+. My opponent gave me a lesson on the board that was just as instructive as the hours of adjournment analysis. We also found some interesting ideas in the post-mortem, where Grandmaster Shamkovich's excellent technique drew rave reviews.

STEP SIX
Lessons Learned

At this point you've seen enough of my terrible moves. Those were not my only errors at the chessboard, just a sample of the ones I consider instructive. To become a Master, and to continue development even beyond that level, you have to learn from your mistakes and try not to repeat them too often!

In each of the following games, errors made in the previous games were, for the most part, avoided. As a result, I was able to defeat many high-ranked players. My peak FIDE rating was 2370, and the majority of my opponents in the games below were ranked considerably higher than that. I want all of my readers to know that if you apply yourself, you can defeat much stronger opposition, or at least avoid losses. This is true even when your opponent is a Grandmaster!

Most of the games were played in professional competition. I include one early simul game, because it is instructive and it remains one of my favorites. Also, I feel an obligation to keep the game in circulation as my opponent tried to suppress it and keep it out of the *New York Times*. He failed.

Otherwise, the opposition includes a number of United States champions and some familiar names from the chess world. Though losing to me, or even allowing me to get away with a draw may have been painful for them at the time, over the years I've taken enough heads to reduce the stigma. In many cases, they outplayed me in one or two phases of the game, only to let me escape and in some cases take revenge.

In some games, I simply had the necessary inspiration to find the solution and the technique, acquired from previous lessons on the receiving end, to carry out the plan.

The games have been chosen for their instructive value, and aren't in any sense a best games collection. Artistic merit isn't the point here, though I am sure you will find many of these games entertaining. At the very least, I hope they inspire you to go out and play your best against your most formidable opposition!

We start with a couple of examples of good opening preparation. Garry Kasparov, the 13th World Champion, is known for his obsession with pre-game preparation. Amateur players cannot afford to devote such time and resources to the task. Still, in openings that are not the most popular, it is possible to prepare thoroughly, especially if you are familiar with your opponent's opening preferences.

The first game involves a different sort of preparation, where an intended night away from the chessboard turns out to be far from chess-free, but inspiring enough to produce a gem the next day.

One approach, seen in some games, is to play confrontationally and optimistically. Another is to play very solidly, waiting for the opponent to slip up while avoiding complications. Many players don't have sufficient confidence to adopt that approach, but remember, if you don't make a mistake, neither Grandmaster nor supercomputer can defeat you!

Most players are quite happy to escape from a Grandmaster encounter with a draw, and that's not easy to achieve. With cautious play it is possible to get to an even endgame, but professionals have spent years developing endgame skills. Having a "drawish" endgame means that the Grandmaster will likely play for as long as it takes for you to make a mistake. Even games that are known as technical draws are often won by the more experienced players.

There are lessons in each stage of the game, from the opening to the endgame. I've tried to include a bit of background for the games, so that you can get a sense of the atmosphere, and appreciate the scale of the upsets.

OPENING PREPARATION

As I've already mentioned, I was fascinated by opening theory when I was a young player. Even in my earliest Junior High School games, I used to play the Closed Variation of the Spanish game 15-16 moves deep. I studied the Najdorf out to move 25 in some lines, which was very deep at the time.

Although most of my openings were quite standard and orthodox, as they should be for a young player, I did like to explore sidelines and forgotten variations. I figured that an opening novelty would be even more effective if played in a line of standard opening. The surprise value would be combined with an assumption that a low rated kid could come up with a good new move.

In the next game, I knew I would play Black, since it was a simultaneous exhibition. I anticipated that if Reshevsky opened 1.d4, I could get to a line of the Queen's Gambit that seemed to me to offer all of the advantages of the Gruenfeld Defense with none of the drawbacks. And I had a little surprise ready.

1.d4 d5; 2.c4 dxc4; 3.Nf3 Nf6; 4.e3 g6. Then, as now, the Smyslov Variation was little more than a footnote in most books. **5.Bxc4 Bg7; 6.0–0 0–0; 7.Nc3 Nfd7; 8.Qe2.** 8.e4 Nb6; 9.Be2 Bg4; 10.Be3 Nc6 was played in Evans-Smyslov, Helsinki Olympiad 1952, which was a game I had studied in preparation for this contest. Black has a lot of pressure on the center. Play continued 11.d5 Bxf3; 12.Bxf3 Ne5; 13.Be2 Nec4 with pressure on the long diagonal. After 14.Bc1 c6!, Black had a strong game.

8...Nb6; 9.Bb3.

Position after 9. Bb3

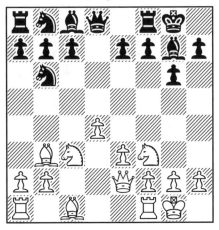

Reschevsky vs. Schiller, Simultaneous Exhibition
Manhattan Chess Club, 1972

9...Nc6!? My earliest theoretical novelty of significance. I knew Reshevsky would choose the normal lines of the Queen's Gambit. Accepted and once into the rare Smyslov system with ...g6 there isn't much room for deviation. My move was an attempt to improve on Golombek - Smyslov, Budapest 1952, which saw 9...a5. **10.Rd1 Bg4; 11.h3 Bxf3; 12.Qxf3 Qe8.**

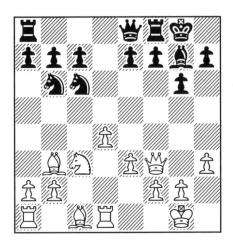

This move has the goal of blasting open the center. After the king moves to the h-file, Black can advance both e- and f-pawns. **13.Nb5?!** Gligoric improved against me a week or two later with 13.Ne4!, with the threat of Nc5. Serves me right for getting the game published in the New York Times! **13...Rc8; 14.Bd2 a6; 15.Na3 Kh8; 16.Rac1 e5!; 17.d5 e4; 18.Qf4.** Now it is clear that the Nc6 is headed for e5, with the possibility of jumping into f3. If only the g-file were open and a rook stood on g8, I could really get things going. I decided to open some lines. **18...g5!; 19.Qxg5 Ne5; 20.Bc3.**

Position after 20.Bc3

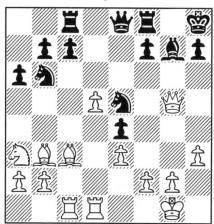

The pin looks strong. But checks have been known to break pins! **20...Nf3+!!; 21.gxf3 Bxc3; 22.Kh1.** On 22.bxc3 Rg8; 23.Qxg8+ Qxg8+; 24.Kh1. 24...Qg6 gives Black a great game. **22...Rg8; 23.Qf4 Qd7; 24.Qh4 Qf5!** Black continues to make threats while improving the position of his queen, before capturing the pawn at b2. **25.f4 Bxb2; 26.Rg1 Bxc1; 27.Rxc1 Qg6; 28.Qg4 Qxg4; 29.hxg4 Rxg4.** White could have resigned here but played on another dozen moves. Then he asked Al Horowitz, the New York Times columnist and Manhattan Chess Club regular, not to publish the game.

But Horowitz, who gave me a few lessons at the club, put it in, much to the delight of a 17-year old chessplayer who had defeated his first Grandmaster, even if it was only a simul.

GAME LESSON THIRTY-EIGHT
To get the game going in your direction, prepare your openings in advance.

PREPARE DEEPLY!

The preparation in the previous game was not particularly deep. I had developed the idea of ...Nc6 in combination with a strategic goal of ...e5. In the next game, the planning had to be far more detailed, and I had to guess at what my opponent, one of the world's leading opening specialists at the time, had planned for me. This is part science, but larger part intuition. When you know your opponent, you can try to put yourself in the position of preparing against the possibilities.

1.d4 d5; 2.Nc3 c6; 3.e4 dxe4; 4.Nxe4 Bf5; 5.Ng3.

I reckoned that he'd try either 5.Nc5 or something in the main lines. I know that Keene is a fan of the Caro for Black, but not the Classical lines. What would he use for inspiration?

5...Bg6; 6.h4 h6; 7.Nf3 Nd7; 8.h5 Bh7; 9.Bd3 Bxd3; 10.Qxd3 Ngf6; 11.Bf4 Qa5+; 12.Bd2 Qc7; 13.Qe2 e6; 14.0-0-0 0-0-0. The old main line. These days I castle on the kingside.

My preparation for this game mostly concentrated on flank openings, because Keene is an authority on those, but I had a suspicion that Ray might want to tackle my Caro-Kann. He really needed a win, as he was not doing well in the round-robin tournament.

15.Ne5 Nxe5; 16.dxe5 Nd7; 17.f4 Be7; 18.Be3!?

Position after 18.Be3!?

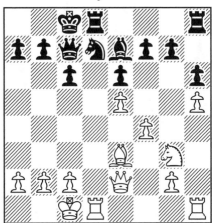

*Keene vs. Schiller, Windy City Invitational
Chicago, 1985*

As one of the main chess advisors to my publisher at the time, Batsford, Keene knew that I had translated many books and articles by Kasparov.

He also knew I didn't have a hand in the book that Kasparov and Shakarov wrote on the Caro-Kann, though I was probably familiar with much of it. He found a new idea, a suggestion by Kasparov in a little note, which claimed an advantage for White. Why not go with Garry's idea?

As it happened, I was more than a little familiar with the move. My copy of the book had a little note I scribbled in the margin which read: 18...Qa5! =. I definitely did not agree that the position favored White in any significant way.

I was delighted when the position arose at the board, and for once had no problem remembering my analysis.

18...Qa5!; 19.Kb1 Nc5; 20.c3. As expected. Now the rooks leave the stage.

20...Rxd1+; 21.Rxd1 Rd8; 22.Rxd8+ Qxd8; 23.Bxc5 Bxc5.

Position after 23...Bxc5

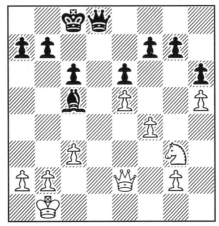

I was out of preparation now, but was certain I could hold the position. Out of respect for his position in the tournament, I didn't insult him with a draw offer. **24.Ne4 Qd5.**

GAME LESSON THIRTY-NINE

If you have already learned the basic opening lines extend your knowledge deeply in lines that are popular or are recommended in books.

Why give up the bishop? Why not, as the exchange leads to an easily drawn queen endgame. **25.Kc2 Be7; 26.b3 Qa5; 27.Kb2 Qb6; 28.Qf2.** Keene's endgame analysis skills have been demonstrated to me time and time again as we have worked together a lot. He is a tremendous analyst. Of course the minor piece endgame is fine for Black, but keeping queens on the board is easier. **28...Qa6; 29.c4 Qa3+; 30.Kb1 Qb4!** The exclamation point is for psychological effect. Instead of cowardly retreating to a5, protecting the pawn, I keep my queen's eye on d6, a more dangerous square. The a-pawn can't be taken because of ...Qe1+. Indeed, Keene could not find any useful plan and offered a draw when I returned to the board. I accepted.

INSPIRATION AS PREPARATION

There are many ways to prepare for a game, but the next game shows that sometimes inspiration comes from an odd direction. Sometimes the most appropriate preparation is to simply relax. If your opening is well prepared and your opponent is not unfamiliar, much of the decision-making takes place away from a chessboard.

The game was played at the San Mateo International Futurity, an internationally ranked chess tournament featuring local masters and masters from Finland and Spain as well as the most promising young stars from Northern California.

With two tough games scheduled for Sunday, a night off at Shoreline Amphitheater for a Phish concert seemed just the right thing to do to relax before the difficult confrontation against the runner-up in the year's Denker Tournament of High School Champions. Adrian Keatinge-Clay, heading to Stanford, was a master seeking to move up into the international ranks.

Since the pressure was on him to earn his international ranking, which I already had, I chose to relax. Chess was far from my mind as I entered the lawn to enjoy my first live Phish show. What greeted me was a strange sight indeed. On the left side of the stage, there was a huge chessboard, with all the pieces in their proper places. I had no idea what was going on, but escaping from chess might prove impossible.

After the first two songs, the band explained what was going on. They are all big fans of the Royal Game and spend a lot of time on the road doing battle at the chessboard. They would be challenging the audience to a game of chess on this national tour, with one move played at each concert.

To get things going, they played a couple of moves. The game began with keyboardist and vocalist Page McConnell using the normal move 1.e4 and a fan by the name of Pooh (I am not sure about the spelling) responded sensibly with

1...e5. Then Page played his pet move 2.Bb5!?, which is the unorthodox opening known as the Portuguese Opening. Pooh took no chances, but slid the game into more orthodox paths with 2...Nc6, and Page responded 3.Nf3, with the game now in the familiar Ruy Lopez Opening (Spanish Game). These moves were made to the accompaniment of White Rabbit.

During the set break, people were invited to gather at the Greenpeace booth and vote on the audience move. Of course I headed there, and introduced myself as a professional and current champion of Northern California. Many moves were suggested by the public.

I explained why I felt that the choice should be between 3...a6 (which has been seen in half the games of the Intel-sponsored PCA World Championship then underway in New York), and 3...Nf6. Eventually 3...a6 was selected by vote.

I was then asked to make the move on the stage, which sounded like fun, so I readily agreed. I was escorted backstage where I met Page, Mike Gordon, Trey Anastasio and Jon Fishman, who are the members of Phish.

They are real chess "phans," and I was happy to discover this, because chess suffers from such a geeky image that to find brilliant and imaginative alternative music performers with a love for the game is really rewarding.

Just before the second set began, I walked on stage alone to make the chosen move before at least 15,000 screaming fans. That might be a record for people in attendance at a chess game!

Unfortunately, the complete game, which took place over period of months in locales scattered throughout the country, was not recorded for posterity. I wasn't able be at the other West Coast concerts, because I was moderating the World Championship coverage on the Internet Chess Club.

On Sunday, I played truly inspired chess to win my match, creating one of my most satisfying games. It involved a huge, long sacrifice that required 15 moves by each player to resolve itself, and I think it is fair to say that my experience at the show played a large part in putting me in the all-important frame of mind necessary to creative play. At the point in the game just before I delivered the decisive sacrifice, I had that same feeling that many of us get when absorbed in great music.

There is the fantastic Zen-like feeling that everything makes sense, that all truth is suddenly revealed even if it cannot be articulated. For those of us who love chess, it is this, not the mere defeating of an opponent that matters. This is why we play, why we devote countless hours to studying the mysteries of the game, which even after 1500 years or so have not been worked out by man or machine. And now for the game...

1.d4 Nf6; 2.c4 g6; 3.Nc3 d5; 4.cxd5 Nxd5; 5.Qb3.
Slightly off the beaten path. This is a line Jon Tisdall showed me about a decade ago. **5...Nxc3; 6.bxc3 Bg7; 7.Nf3 0–0; 8.e3.** This solid approach is my own idea. It doesn't promise White much, but I am content to let the game develop slowly.

8...c5; 9.Ba3 b6; 10.Rd1 Qc7.

Position after 10... Qc7

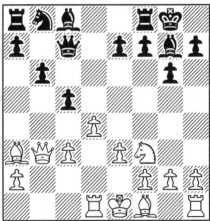

Schiller vs. Keatinge-Clay,
San Mateo International Futurity, 1995

11.Bc4?! A poor choice. I just should have settled for 11.Be2. On c4 the bishop is too exposed. **11...Nc6!** Threatening ...Na5, attacking my queen and bishop.

12.Bd5 e6; 13.Bxc6 Qxc6; 14.0–0 Ba6; 15.Rfe1 Rfd8; 16.Rd2 Rac8; 17.e4 cxd4; 18.cxd4.

This is the position I was aiming for, but I underestimated how weak my pawn at a2 is.

18...Bc4; 19.Qe3 Rc7; 20.Red1 Qa4; 21.Rc1 a5; 22.Rdc2 b5; 23.Bc5! Rdc8; 24.Bd6 Rc6; 25.Bf4.

Position after 25.Bf4

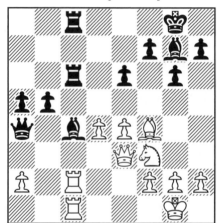

The plan was to get the bishop to the kingside, where it might do some good. I begin to sense some real attacking possibilities, but nothing concrete.

25...f6; 26.h4. An important move, making room for my king and adding pressure on the kingside.

This pawn plays a crucial role in the final combination.

26...Bf8.

Position after 26...Bf8

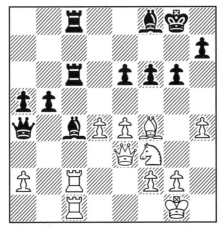

This is a critical position. Now the sacrifices begin. **27.d5!** This will lead to the loss of the exchange. But I have most of the rest of the game worked out, except for one detail. **27... Bxd5; 28.exd5 Rxc2; 29.Qxe6+ Kg7; 30.Rxc2 Rxc2.** Taking with the queen would not have made a big difference. **31.Qd7+ Kg8; 32.Qe6+.** I am just marking time for a few minutes to collect my thoughts. The key idea still eludes my calculations. **32...Kg7.**

Position after 32...Kg7

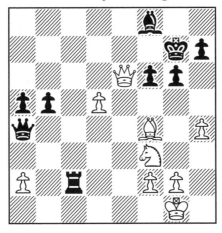

At this point the Zen-like light dawned, the incredible feeling of having the answers to all the questions, of seeing the clear path to victory. The advance of my pawn from f2-f4 was hidden in the fog, and looking at the position you can see why: f4 is occupied by a bishop, and the knight is in the way.

But the truth rushed in from all sides, and I couldn't keep a little smile from peeking through.

33.Qd7+ Kg8; 34.Ng5!!

Position after 34.Ng5!!

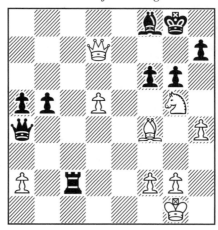

This move forces victory.

34...fxg5. Black has to capture because of the threats at f7 and h7, e.g., 34...Bg7; 35.Qf7+ Kh8; 36.Qe8+ Bf8; 37.Qxf8#.

35.Qe6+ Kg7. 35...Kh8 is dealt with efficiently by 36.Be5+ Bg7; 37.Qe8#. **36.Be5+ Kh6; 37.hxg5+ Kh5.** Black also loses if he captures the pawn. 37...Kxg5; 38.Bf6+ Kf4; 39.Qe5+ Kg4; 40.Qg5#.

38.Qh3+ Kxg5. 38...Qh4; 39.g4+ Kxg5; 40.f4+ Kh6; 41.Qxh4#. **39.f4+!**

Position after 39.f4+!

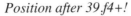

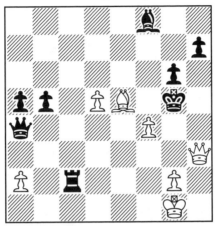

This is the point I had to see back at move 32. I didn't notice the possibility when I started the combination back at move 27. But even at move 32, I had this worked out through move 45.

39...Qxf4; 40.Bxf4+ Kxf4; 41.Qf3+ Ke5; 42.Qxf8 Kxd5. The rook is no match for the queen, even with two extra pawns. The pawns fall like ripe apples. **43.Qd8+ Kc4; 44.Qxa5 b4; 45.Qc7+ Kd3; 46.Qd6+ Kc4; 47.Qc6+ Kd3; 48.Qd5+ Kc3; 49.Qb3+ Kd2; 50.Qxb4+** Black could have resigned here, or earlier, but he was still trying to figure out what had gone so terribly wrong. **50...Ke2; 51.Qe4+ Kd2; 52.Qxc2+!**

GAME LESSON FORTY
Go into a game in a good mood, and inspiration will flow.

A final queen sacrifice to end the game with a flourish. After the Black king captures the queen, the a-pawn simply marches up the board until I get a new one. So Adrian resigned.

THE ROUNDABOUT ATTACK

Sometimes the best way into an enemy position is to sneak around back. Pieces slide to the flank across the board from the target, work their way into the enemy home ranks, and then strike from the side. Rooks and queens work best for this sort of operation. In this game, the rooks start with a frontal assault but find the front door locked, so the roundabout strategy is used.

1.d4 d5; 2.c4 e6; 3.Nf3 c6; 4.Nbd2 f5; 5.g3 Nf6; 6.Bg2 Bd6; 7.0–0 Qe7; 8.Qc2 0–0; 9.Ne5 Nbd7; 10.Ndf3.

Position after 10.Ndf3

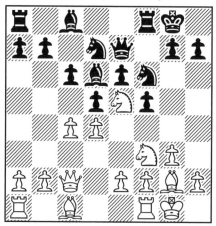

D. Gurevich vs. Schiller, Played in Oak Brook, 1993

This is a standard anti-Dutch plan. The knight at e5 is supported by both a pawn at d4 and another knight at either f3 or d3.

10...Ne4. Black can safely keep the knight here if an enemy knight is at f3, so that White cannot place a pawn there. In many cases the knight can sit at e4 even if the f3-square is not occupied, since the weakening of the a7-g1 diagonal can prove embarrassing for White if the f-pawn advances.

In addition, g3 can become vulnerable. **11.Bf4.** White invites Black to advance the g-pawn. This is a double-edged strategy. **11...g5!?** Black accepts the challenge. **12.Nxd7 Bxd7; 13.Bxd6 Nxd6.** White now owns a superior bishop, but Black has plenty of room to maneuver. **14.Ne5 Be8.** There are two ways to activate the light-squared bishop in the Stonewall Dutch. Black can fianchetto it at b7 under some circumstances, most easily when the knight sits at b8 to defend the pawn at c6. The other plan, seen here, is to redeploy it on the kingside. **15.f4.** 15.c5 Nf7; 16.Nxf7 Bxf7; 17.f3 Bg6; 18.e4 f4 leaves White with more problems to solve than Black. **15...Bh5; 16.Rac1 Rac8; 17.Kh1.** White takes care to get the king off the a7-g1 diagonal in case Black opens up the game with ...c5.

17...Nf7.

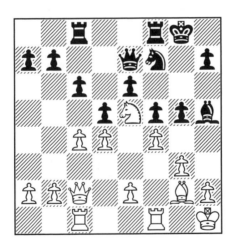

18.cxd5 exd5. 18...cxd5 allows White to sacrifice the queen, though moving her to a safe square is also good. 19.Qxc8 Rxc8; 20.Rxc8+ Kg7; 21.Rfc1 Qb4; 22.fxg5 Nxe5; 23.dxe5 Qxb2; 24.R1c7+ Bf7; 25.Bf3! and White wins. **19.e3 Nxe5!** Although Black has a bad bishop, there is little to fear in most of the possible endgames. **20.fxe5 Bg6.**

White must now take seriously the threat of advancing the f-pawn. **21.Qd2 Kg7.** Black prepares to operate on the h-file. **22.b4 h5; 23.Rf2 Rh8; 24.Rcf1 h4!; 25.Kg1.** White gets the king off the dangerous h-file. **25...g4; 26.Rc1 Qg5; 27.Rf4.** White does not want to allow ...f4, even as a sacrifice. **27...Rh7; 28.b5 hxg3; 29.hxg3 Qh5.**

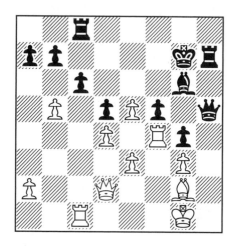

30.Qf2? This square is needed for the king. 30.Kf2 threatens Rh1, trapping the enemy queen. 30...Qh2; 31.Rh1. Forced, in view of the threat of ...Rh3. 31...Qxh1; 32.Bxh1 Rxh1; 33.Qb4 cxb5; 34.Kg2 Rch8; 35.Qe7+ Bf7; 36.Qf6+ Kf8; 37.Qd8+ Kg7; 38.Qf6+ would have drawn. **30...Qh2+; 31.Kf1 Rhh8!**

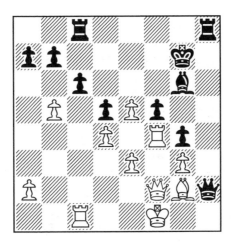

It looks as though Black cannot make further progress. It is true that I have exhausted the possibilities on the h-file, but there is another path to the enemy king, via the queenside, and with the next very subtle move I prepare a deep and long plan. **32.bxc6.** Had Dmitry figured out the point of my last move, he never would have opened up the b-file.

32.Rb1 b6; 33.bxc6 Rxc6; 34.Bxd5 Rc2; 35.Qxh2 Rhxh2 leaves White too tied down to make any progress.

32...Rxc6; 33.Rxc6 bxc6; 34.Qe1. 34.Qc2 Rb8; 35.Kf2 Rb6 and again White has no way to make progress. **34...Rb8; 35.a4 Rb3!** White is completely tied down.

36.Rf2. Desperation. The rook should stay in its passive post at f4, as now the Black bishop enters the game. 36.a5 Rb7 and White is at a loss for a move, as all of the pieces must remain in place to defend.

36...f4!

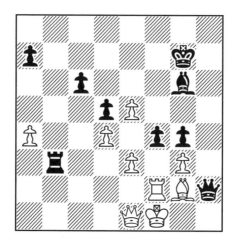

The deadly threat is ...Rb1. **37.Rd2 Rxe3; 38.Qf2 Qxg3; 39.Qxg3 Rxg3; 40.Rf2 f3; 41.Bh1 Bd3+**. White resigned.

SPECULATIVE PLAY REWARDED - A

The next game is one of my favorites. The sacrifices aren't completely sound, but the game is fascinating in its complexity. It is a good test game for computer chess programs, as some of the ramifications of individual moves are not revealed until many moves have been played. Human players have found it interesting, too. It was played in an early round of one of the famous Regency Masters tournaments, and analysis of the game went on every day until the end of the event.

The Regency Hotel in Ramsgate was owned by Ian Josephs, a chessplayer. He had the presence of mind and goodwill toward his fellows to use the hotel to host a school for foreigners, mostly young women, to learn English. The playing hall was right next to the bar, and the disco was distracting a number of chessplayers there, but no one complained.

Indeed, those of us who had to brave the storm to get to Brighton for the next tournament had many reasons to regret our departure as our driver (trains were shut down) attempted to drive in heavy snow for the first time. To keep distracted, the passengers devoted considerable time to further analysis of the game!

Speculative play is not like gambit play. A gambit has a specific goal, usually rapid development, with reasonable possibilities to recover the sacrificed material. In speculative play, the sacrifice is usually permanent. The complications are not worked out in advance, though a few appealing tactical lines usually have floated to the surface.

It mustn't be a bluff, as the sacrifice has to lead to very concrete positional factors, which give confidence to the attacking side. The pace of attack does not have to be fast, it just has to be faster than the enemy's defense. Most speculative sacrifices take place when enemy pieces are offside and cannot quickly rush to the aid of the king.

1.e4 c5; 2.Nc3. This move is not necessarily an invitation to the Closed Variations or Grand Prix Attack. Instead, it is an attempt to transpose into a normal Open Sicilian, which normally is reached via 2.Nf3. Therefore Black must be careful to choose a reply which keeps open the possibilities of transposing into the main lines.

2...e6; 3.Nge2 d6; 4.d4 cxd4. Now we have reached the standard positions in the opening. **5.Nxd4 a6.** The Najdorf Variation is one of Black's most popular options, and it will be reached after Black plays ...Nf6.

6.Be3 Nf6; 7.g4. This move transposes to systems that usually arise after 6.g4, known as the Keres Attack. Transposing back into the normal lines by playing either 7...h6 or 7...Nc6 is possible. My opponent reasons that there is another possibility that suggests itself because of the position of the bishop.

7...h5. In fact, the same reasoning led Swedish Grandmaster Ulf Andersson to the same conclusion back in the 1970s, and both played the same reply, advancing the pawn to h5. This entire system is very popular now, but few players seem to be aware of its history. At the Groningen GM Open of 1996, one Grandmaster excitedly showed me his "new idea" with ...h5 and I had to burst his bubble.

Position after 7...h5

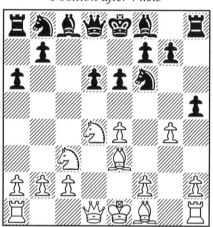

Schiller vs. Paolozzi, Regency Masters Ramsgate England, 1981

7...h6 transposes to more normal Keres Attack lines, though these are by no means harmless for Black.

8.g5 Ng4; 9.Bc1 Qb6. This is a departure from the plan adopted by Andersson, but it is not bad. Black zooms in on the dark squares.

10.h3 Ne5; 11.Be2 g6; 12.Nb3 Nbc6; 13.f4!? This entails a bit of risk, exposing a lot of territory near my king. In return, however, I keep the initiative. The obvious alternative was to chase the queen away with Be3. I don't like to chase the queen away from an awkward square. Thematically, Black must strive for ...b5, and that entails moving the queen. So why push it in the right direction? Fifteen years later two top stars pursued that course. 13.Be3 Qc7; 14.f4 Nd7; 15.Qd2 b5; 16.0-0-0 Bb7; 17.Rhf1 Rc8; 18.Bd3 and White does have a rather pleasant position, Almasi-Polgar, Tilburg 1996. Well, I couldn't have known that back in 1981! **13...Nd7; 14.Rf1 Qc7; 15.Be3 b5; 16.f5!?** This is the kind of move you hold your breath while playing. I keep the initiative and weaken the enemy kingside, but I give up control of the e5-square, which is probably the most important square on the board. Speculative moves like this have gotten me into trouble many times, but in this case things worked out well. **16...Nde5; 17.Nd4 Bd7.** 17...Nxd4; 18.Bxd4 is risky for Black. White threatens to capture at e5, establishing a queenside pawn majority. For example, 18...b4; 19.fxg6 bxc3; 20.gxf7+ Nxf7; 21.Rxf7! Qxf7; 22.Bxh8 and the threat of Be2xh5 is terrible to behold. On the other hand, 17...b4; 18.fxg6 bxc3; 19.gxf7+ Nxf7; 20.Nxc6 cxb2; 21.Rb1 Qxc6; 22.Bxh5 creates the nasty threat of g6 followed by g7.

Black will have to return material and is left with a dangerously exposed king. 22...Qxe4; 23.Bxf7+ Ke7; 24.Qf3 Qxf3; 25.Rxf3 Bg7; 26.g6 Bf6; 27.c3! is better for White. I didn't see all this at the time, but was confident that whatever Black chose I'd have good attacking chances especially if the f-file could be ripped open.

18.fxe6 fxe6.

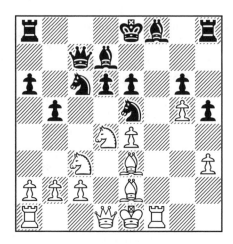

19.Rf6! This move is stronger than it looks. Many humans would reject it quickly, since the rook will be chased away before it can do any harm. I had my eyes on the weak kingside pawns. **19...Nd8.** Now all Black needs to do is play ...Be7 and the White rook will have to retreat, leaving White with an inferior game. Or so it seems. I didn't hesitate to sacrifice the rook.

20.Rxg6! Nxg6; 21.Bxh5 Nf7. This position has been used to test computer evaluation functions. Almost all of the machines fail to find the correct continuations. They do see that 21...Kf7?? loses instantly to 22.Qf3+, but rarely see what White's plan is.

22.Bxg6. This is the only reasonable move. **22...Rxh3.** There is now a nasty threat of ...Rh1+.

Here I slip up in my desperation to keep Black from castling to safety. The correct plan was very hard to see. **23.Bxf7+?!** This is not the most accurate move, since it gives Black more defensive possibilities. I just didn't consider 23.Kd2! This clever, but seemingly reckless move, would have given me a very strong attack. 23...Rh2+. 23...Bc8; 24.Qe2 e5 is the line preferred by many computer programs, and it is absolutely horrible. No human master would advance the e-pawn, because:

a) it means that the Bf8 has no future

b) it critically weakens f5

c) it opens up a huge hole at d5.

25.Nd5 Qb7; 26.Rf1! is very strong. 26...exd4; 27.Rxf7 Qxf7; 28.Bxf7+ Kxf7; 29.Qf1+ Kg8; 30.Bxd4. White wins easily.); 24.Kc1 Bc8; 25.Qf3 Rb8; 26.Bh5 threatens to advance the g-pawn to g6 and then g7, so Black must blockade the g7-square. 26...Bg7; 27.Bg1. Black is in serious trouble. White has so many threats it is not clear that Black can survive. **23... Kxf7.**

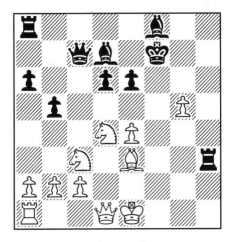

24.Qe2!? Here I could have played my king to d2 instead, but I had hopes of castling to bring my king to safety on the kingside.

24...Qc4?! This move is an obvious attempt to exchange queens, and would be played by most players. White's resources are buried quite deeply and are hard to find, especially in a tournament situation. Accepting the double-rook sacrifice with 24...Rh1+ would lead to a very long series of relatively forced moves.

I only present the main line: 25.Kd2 Rxa1; 26.Qh5+ Ke7; 27.Nf5+! exf5; 28.Nd5+ Kd8; 29.Qf7 Kc8; 30.Qxf8+ Kb7; 31.Qxa8+! Kxa8; 32.Nxc7+ Kb7; 33.Nd5. This was as far as my mind could take me at the time. I had confidence that the g-pawn was worth the exchange (rook vs knight). **25.Qf2+.** Exchanging queens is certainly out of the question. **25...Kg8; 26.g6 Bg7?** A time-pressure error. 26...Rh1+?; 27.Kd2 Rxa1?! loses to 28.Qf7+ Kh8; 29.Qh7#, but 26...Be8 was safer, guarding the critical f7-square. **27.Qf7+ Kh8; 28.0–0–0!** It was finally time to castle! **28...Be8.**

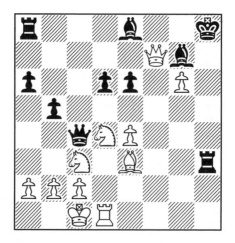

Now what can White do? 28...Rxe3 loses to 29.Rh1+. **29.Qxe6!!** An amazing move, because we see a violation of the most basic attacking principle: Don't exchange the powerful queens when attacking. It also violates the near-cardinal rule: don't exchange pieces when you are behind in material!

I showed this game to Garry Kasparov a few months later at the super tournament in Bugojno. It gave me considerable pleasure that even Garry Kasparov couldn't find this in four minutes although he had recently been awarded Grandmaster in 1981, and was just starting his climb to the championship.

He recommended the game for inclusion in the Chess Informant series and it was published in volume 33.

29...Qxe6. 29...Rxe3; 30.Rh1+ wins for White. **30.Nxe6 Rxe3?** Black could simply capture at g6 instead, but failed to see why the fruit at e3 is forbidden. 30...Bxc3! is the best move, and then Black will wind up at least the exchange. Black was in severe time trouble already, which made it hard to evaluate the endgames; for example: 31.bxc3 Rxe3; 32.Rh1+ Kg8; 33.Rh7, where Black has to stop the eternal harassment of the king with 33...Bxg6.

Then 34.Rg7+ Kh8; 35.Rxg6 Rxe4 leaves Black the exchange up, though a win still requires a fair bit of work. So trading queens was the best chance for White. **31.Rh1+ Kg8; 32.Nd5!**

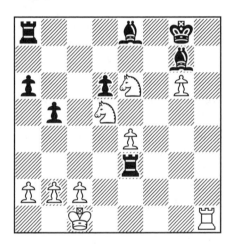

The threat is Ne7 checkmate! **32...Bxg6; 33.Nxe3 Bxe4; 34.Rg1 Ra7; 35.Rg4 Bh7?** A final mistake, with the clock leaving little time to find that 35...d5!; 36.Kd2! d4; 37.Rxe4 dxe3+; 38.Kxe3 Bxb2 would have earned a draw, assuming Black could reach time control.

36.Nd5! This wins by force. Black cannot prevent the liquidation of pieces that leads to a winning endgame for White. **36...Kh8; 37.Nxg7 Rxg7; 38.Rxg7 Kxg7.** Any competent player can quickly conclude resignation is inevitable for Black.

39.Nc7. This wins a pawn. **39...Kf6.** If the a-pawn had advanced, then the b-pawn would have fallen. **40.Nxa6 Ke5; 41.Nc7.** My opponent resigned, since if the pawn advances to b4, then the knight returns to a6 attacking it, and any further advance would run into the wall of White pawns. The ending is such a trivial matter that few masters would bother even trying to defend.

GAME LESSON FORTY-TWO

Sacrificing to keep the enemy king in the center often pays off!

SPECULATIVE PLAY REWARDED - B

Speculative play is generally only rewarded when the opponent plays imperfectly, but this happens in most games where the players are flesh and blood. In the next game, more precise defense would have saved the day, but it is tough, even for a Grandmaster!

1.e4. e6; 2.d4 d5; 3.Nc3 Nf6; 4.e5.

The old Steinitz variation is enjoying renewed popularity these days. A game between Kasparov and Short at the 1994 Euwe Memorial in Amsterdam had made a deep impression on me, and I was hoping to make use of a plan involving h4, Rh3-g3 and a kingside attack that worked well for Kasparov.

4...Nfd7; 5.f4 c5; 6.Nf3 Nc6; 7.Be3 Qb6; 8.Qd2.

The pawn sacrifice offered by this move has rarely been tested in the tournament arena. I was quite surprised when Schwartzman accepted it.

8...Qxb2; 9.Rb1 Qa3.

Position after 9...Qa3

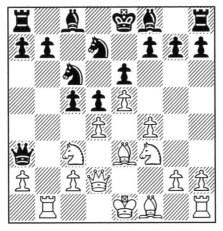

Schiller vs. Schwartzman, U.S. Open
Alexandria VA, 1994

10.dxc5. This was an original idea. 10.Be2 was recommended in an old book by Harding, but it did not impress me at all. I decided to eliminate the dark-squared bishops and use Kasparov's attacking formation on the kingside. **10...Bxc5; 11.Bxc5 Qxc5; 12.Bd3 a6; 13.h4 Nb6.** 13...Qe7 would have made it harder for me to justify the investment of the pawn. **14.Rh3! Nc4; 15.Bxc4 Qxc4; 16.a3!**

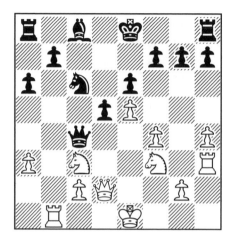

This is a very important move. I need to free the knight from the need to hang around at c3 just to defend the poor pawn.

16...b5; 17.Ne2 Bd7; 18.Nfd4!

This eliminates the enemy knight, and I have a decent endgame even without the pawn, because Black is left with a very bad bishop.

18...Nxd4; 19.Nxd4 Rc8.

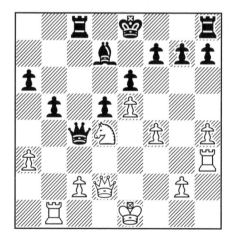

20.Rbb3! There are two points to this move. One is to be ready to transfer to the kingside at a moment's notice, and the other point, more subtle, will be revealed shortly.

20...0–0; 21.Rhg3 f6.

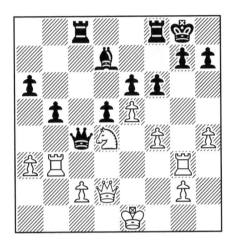

I anticipated this standard French counterplay.

22.f5!? I hadn't worked out all the tactics here, but I had a great deal of confidence and had seen some pleasant long variations, beginning at move 27!

22...exf5. This fell in with my plans. But what about the alternative? Could I have held the position following 22... fxe5; 23.Qh6 Rf7; 24.Rb4 Qc5!; 25.fxe6 Re7!; 26.exd7 exd4+; 27.Kf1 Rf8+; 28.Kg1 d3+; 29.Kh2 Kh8! (Avoiding 29...dxc2? which allows 30.Rbg4! with devastating threats at g7. Another trap is 29...Rxd7; 30.cxd3.); 30.Qf4! Rxd7 (Not 30...Rxf4??, which allows 31.d8Q+.); 31.Qg4 dxc2!; 32.Qxd7 g6, where Black wins. It might not have been easy, but neither would it have been a simple matter to find all these moves at the board!

23.Rbc3!

153

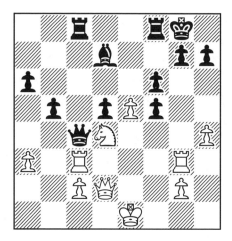

A critical preparatory move before the real attack begins.
23...Qa4; 24.Qh6 Rf7; 25.exf6 g6.

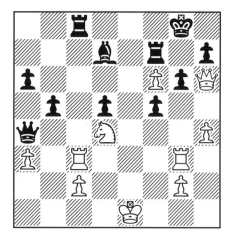

Black is relying on the pawns for protection, but a brutal sacrifice rips open the kingside.

26.Rxg6+!! hxg6; 27.Qxg6+ Kf8. The king can run but he cannot hide.

28.Qh6+ Ke8; 29.Qh8+ Rf8; 30.Re3+ Kd8. One rook must be abandoned, and the other soon follows.

31.Qxf8+ Kc7; 32.Qc5+ Kb8; 33.Qd6+ Rc7; 34.Rc3 Qa5; 35.Qxc7+. Black resigned.

GAME LESSON FORTY-THREE

In sharp positions material isn't as important, so invensting a little to mix things up is often a good idea.

SPECULATIVE PLAY REWARDED - C

As I was finishing writing a book on the games of Rudolf Spielmann, I took part in one of the regular all-Master training tournaments held monthly in the San Francisco area. I found myself paired with a very strong opponent, Mike Arne (2400 FIDE).

Since we were due to meet a few weeks later in an IM norm tournament, I decided that I shouldn't play my special preparation for him. Naturally with so much Spielmann on my mind I turned to one of his favorite lines, the Worral Attack in the Spanish Game. My preparation consisted solely of annotating a few games for my book, and the choice was made at the board. So this game shows that it is not necessary to study a lot of opening theory as White in the Spanish Game. All that is needed is some basic concepts, and either courage or recklessness!

1.e4 e5; 2.Nf3 Nc6; 3.Bb5 a6; 4.Ba4 Nf6; 5.Qe2 b5; 6.Bb3 Bc5. The sharpest continuation. **7.c3 0–0; 8.0–0 d6.** 8... d5 is a good alternative. **9.h3.** This is not necessary, as Black's bishop is headed to b7, but I wanted to make sure it was kept off of g4 where the pin on the knight would weaken my control of d4.

9...Bb7; 10.Rd1 Re8; 11.a4 b4; 12.a5 Qb8?! In retrospect, this is an error. The simple 12...Qe7 would have given Black an equal game.

13.d4!?

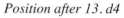

Position after 13. d4

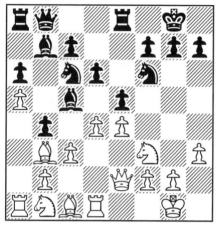

Schiller vs. Arne, Foster City, 1995

This is a speculative sacrifice. I saw the Black forces huddled on the queenside and felt that a pawn could safely be invested for good attacking chances. My bishops will be very strong

13...exd4; 14.cxd4 Ba7. 14...Rxe4 was certainly playable, but I felt that I would then have sufficient compensation after 15.Be3!?

15.e5! One would think that this move would be more dangerous to White, since the Black rook at e8 is lined up against the queen. The goal is to remove the knight from f6, leaving the kingside defended by mere pawns.

15...d5. 15...Nd7; 16.Ng5 would have given White a strong attack. 15...dxe5; 16.dxe5 Nd8; 17.Ng5 threatens Rxd8 followed by an assault at f7. 15...Re7 would have been met by 16.Bg5, which threatens to smash open the kingside.

16.Qd3! Now Black must try for complications. **16...Ne4.** On 16...Nd7; 17.Bxd5 Ne7; 18.Bc4 is simple and strong.

17.Bxd5 Nxf2.

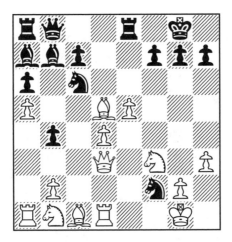

The idea is that if White captures the knight the pin on d4 allows captures at e5 with counterplay. Instead, I sacrifice a bishop and a rook to go after the undefended Black king.

18.Bxf7+!!; 18.Kxf2 Nxe5; 19.Qb3 Bxd5; 20.Qxd5 Nxf3; 21.gxf3 c5 leaves the White king vulnerable to attack.

18...Kxf7; 19.Qf5+ Kg8; 20.Ng5.

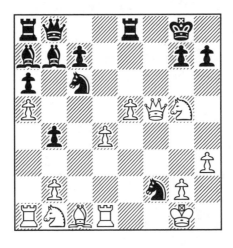

Black might now have tried 20...Nxh3+, which would have required White to find some good moves. 21.Qxh3 Bxd4+!; 22.Rxd4! Nxd4; 23.Qxh7+ keeps the attack going.

157

For example 23...Kf8; 24.Qh8+ Ke7; 25.Qxg7+ Kd8; 26.Be3 Nf5; 27.Qf6+ Ne7; 28.Qe6, or 26...c5; 27.Bxd4 cxd4; 28.Qf6+ Kd7; 29.Qf5+ Kc6; 30.Na3! and the knight cannot be captured because of 31.Rc1+ and mate follows quickly.

Instead, the game continued **20...Nxd1; 21.Qxh7+.**

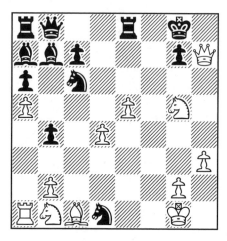

21...Kf8; 22.Qh8+ Ke7; 23.Qxg7+ Kd8; 24.Nf7+ Kd7.

So far, White's moves have been easy. This position looks great for White, but it is not so simple to keep the attack going. After all, Black is ready to take the initiative by capturing at d4 with the bishop, which could then become a useful defensive asset.

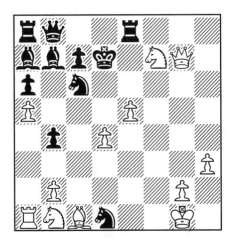

25.e6+! Less effective is 25.Nd6+ Re7; 26.Qg4+ Re6 and unfortunately the d-pawn, being pinned, cannot advance to d5. Nor does 25.Ng5+ do the trick, as Black retreats to c8. The Black pieces come alive on 25.Bg5 Bxd4+; 26.Kh1 Nf2+; 27.Kh2 Ne7, so the pawn had to be sacrificed.

25...Kxe6. Black can't go to c9 because of Nd6+ followed by Qd7#. The next series of moves is forced.

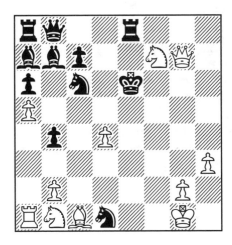

26.Ng5+ Kd5. The Black king runs to daylight. The alternative was 26...Kd6; 27.Bf4+; for example, 27...Ne5; 28.Bxe5 Kc6; 29.Qg6+ Kb5; 30.Na3+ bxa3; 31.Qd3+ Kc6; 32.Rc1+ Kd7; 33.Qf5+ Ke7; 34.Bf6+ Kd6; 35.Nf7#, or 29... Qd8; 30.Bf6+ and mate follows.

27.Qd7+. If the Black king is allowed to capture the d-pawn, then the next time it moves it will expose the White king to check from the bishop at a7, and that may, in some circumstances, give Black enough time to regroup.

27...Kc4; 28.Nd2+ Kd3; 29.Qf5+! Kxd4.

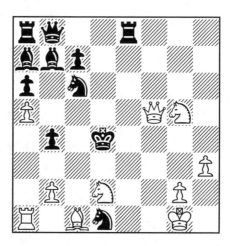

Surely there is a mating net here! There is, but it involves a problem-like move. **30.Ngf3+!** 30.Ndf3+ Kc4+ would have prolonged the game.

30...Ke3; 31.Kf1!! A quiet king move ends the spectacular combination. The final position deserves its own picture.

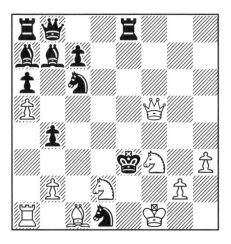

Black resigned, as there is no way out of checkmate.

GAME LESSON FORTY-FOUR

If you want to go king-hunting, you'll need to provide some bait!

SPECULATIVE PLAY REWARDED - D

1.d4 d5; 2.Nf3 Nf6; 3.e3 e6; 4.Bd3 Be7; 5.0–0 0–0; 6.Nbd2 Nbd7; 7.b3 Re8; 8.Bb2 a5; 9.Ne5 a4; 10.f4 Nf8; 11.Ndf3 Ne4; 12.Ng5!?

Position after 12. Ng5

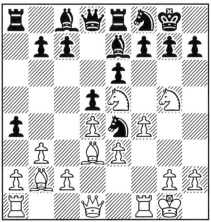

Schiller vs. Ionescu, Zemitis International Futurity,
San Francisco, 2000

Our final example of speculative play rewarded involves not only the offer of a pawn, but in a circumstance where another pawn, the weakling at e3, will be offered as well. **12...Bxg5.** Black could also have captured with the knight, but White comes out on top after 12...Nxg5; 13.fxg5 Bxg5; 14.Nxf7 Bxe3+; 15.Kh1 Qe7; 16.Qe2 Bg5; 17.Nxg5 Qxg5; 18.Qf3.

The best defense was 12...Nd6!, but after 13.Ba3!? Black would be faced with a difficult decision. Capturing at b3 is unwise. The pawn will eat its way to the promotions square, but in the meantime, White inflicts too much damage: 13...axb3; 14.Bxd6 b2; 15.Ngxf7 bxa1Q; 16.Qxa1 cxd6; 17.Nxd8 dxe5; 18.Nxe6 Bxe6; 19.fxe5 and Black is in serious trouble. Black must also be careful to avoid further weakening the kingside. 13...f6; 14.Qh5! g6; 15.Nxg6 hxg6; 16.Bxg6 fxg5; 17.Bxd6 cxd6; 18.Bf7+ Kg7; 19.fxg5!

Accepting the pawn at g5 leads to the most complicated variations. 13...Bxg5; 14.fxg5 Qxg5; 15.Bxd6 cxd6; 16.Nxf7 Qxe3+; 17.Kh1 e5; 18.Qh5 remains murky. Black can try either 18...g6 or 18...Re7, but faces a difficult defense in either case. White's attack is worth more than a pawn.

13.fxg5 Qxg5; 14.Bxe4 Qxe3+. Black could insert 14...f6; 15.Bd3, but after 15...Qxe3+; 16.Kh1 fxe5; 17.dxe5, White still has a strong game.

15.Kh1 Qxe4; 16.Rxf7.

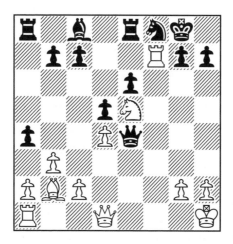

White's powerful knight and invading rook don't have much support, but don't need any. Black's pieces remain useless, while White's rush in.

16...Nd7. Getting rid of White's knight is a sensible plan. **17.Qh5.** Less clear is 17.Rxd7 Bxd7; 18.Nxd7 b6. **17...Nxe5; 18.dxe5 axb3; 19.Raf1.** It looks as though White could make progress with 19.Rxc7 Rf8; 20.Qg5, but after 20...Qg6; 21.Qxg6 hxg6; 22.cxb3, Black has 22...Rxa2!

19...Qg6; 20.Qf3. Exchanging queens fails to achieve the objective. On 20.Qxg6 hxg6; 21.axb3 Ra2; 22.Bc3 Rxc2; 23.Rxc7 b6; 24.h3 Rd8; 25.Rff7, Black defends with 25...Rd7!

20...Bd7!

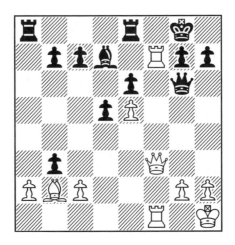

An excellent resource, since capturing on d7 allows Black to get a rook to f8. Control of that square is crucial.

21.Ba3! h6; 22.Bf8 Rxf8, or 22...bxa2; 23.Rxg7+ Qxg7; 24.Bxg7 Kxg7; 25.Qf7+ Kh8; 26.Ra1 Bb5; 27.Qg6, with a tremendous game for White.

23.Rxf8+ Rxf8; 24.Qxf8+ Kh7; 25.cxb3 Bb5; 26.Rg1 c6?! Black misses a bitter defense. 26...Bd3!; 27.Qe7 Be4; 28.Qb4 (28.Qxc7? Bxg2+; 29.Rxg2 Qb1+; 30.Rg1 Qe4+=); 28...b6; 29.Qd4 c5 is unclear.

27.Qb4 Qe4? Badly misjudging the endgame. It is too late to plant the bishop: 27...Bd3; 28.Qxb7 Be4 runs into 29.Qb6! A reasonable practical try is 27...Qf5; 28.a4 Ba6, but even here White is better.

For example, 29.Qd6 Bf1; 30.Qb4 Qf2; 31.h3! Avoiding the trap seen in the previous note. 31...Ba6; 32.Qg4 with a very strong game. The endgame, which follows the exchange of queens, is easily won if played properly.

28.Qxe4+ dxe4; 29.Re1 Bd3; 30.g4!+.

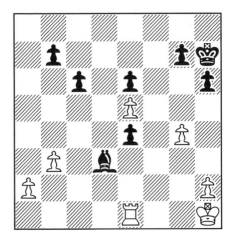

That's the move my opponent failed to consider when he allowed the queen swap. Although the g-pawn seems to be vulnerable, it will soon enjoy the direct protection of the king.

GAME LESSON FORTY-FIVE
A weak backward pawn can be sacrificed for the initiative.

30...h5. Black hopes White will capture, after which ... Kh6 will recover the pawn.

31.Kg2! h4. Black needs to decline the pawn, since after 31...hxg4; 32.Kg3 Kg6; 33.Kxg4 Kh6; 34.Kf4, Black has nothing better than g5+; 35.Ke3 Kg6; 36.Rg1. White will inevitably infiltrate on the kingside; for example, Kf5; 37.Rg2 Bb1; 38.Kd4 Kf4; 39.Rf2+ Kg4; 40.b4 Kh3; 41.a4 g4; 42.a5 g3; 43.hxg3 Kxg3; 44.Rf7 etc.

32.Kh3! g5. Forced. Now the kingside is closed.

33.Kg2 c5; 34.Rc1 b6; 35.Kf2 Kg7; 36.a4 c4; 37.bxc4. Black resigned.

PATIENCE! - A

The games below show how patient, accurate play can lead to success even against Grandmaster opposition in serious tournament play. The games start out innocently enough using the Reti Opening, a system I have adopted in many important games. Although the opening has a reputation for being rather quiet, it can build into an aggressive queenside campaign.

I chose the opening because it is very hard to defeat without taking some risk. The burden of attack is on Black, since White can pursue queenside ambitions easily.

1.Nf3 d5; 2.c4 d4; 3.b4 g6; 4.Bb2 Bg7; 5.g3 a5; 6.a3 e5; 7.d3 Ne7; 8.Bg2 c5; 9.Qb3 axb4; 10.axb4 Rxa1; 11.Bxa1 Nbc6.

Position after 11.Nbc6

Schiller vs. D. Gurevich, Mechanics Masters San Francisco, 1997

The game has developed rather quietly. I had to consider carefully the consequences of my next move. Advancing the b-pawn secures a great advantage if I can later take control of the a-file.

However, opening up the a5-e1 diagonal has some risk attached. The complications are not hard to analyze tactically, but the evaluation of the resulting positions isn't easy. **12.b5.** The contour of the game is established. Black has a weak pawn at b6. This can be a mantra for White. Just repeat it over and over and remember that in the end, that pawn at b6 is the key target. **12...Qa5+; 13.Nfd2 Nb4.** 13...Qxa1; 14.bxc6 Nxc6; 15.0–0 is very unclear. **14.Bb2 0–0; 15.0–0 b6; 16.Na3 Qa7; 17.Ra1!** Ownership of the a-file is crucial. The remainder of the middlegame requires patient play, taking care to meet all enemy threats while preparing the invasion via the a-file. **17...Qb8; 18.Nc2 Nxc2; 19.Qxc2 Bg4.** Black tries to get some counterplay. **20.Nf1 h5; 21.h3 Be6; 22.Qa4 Qd6; 23.Bc1 h4!** A good move, but this was an offer I didn't have to refuse. **24.Qa7?!** Should have just captured at h4. **24...f5; 25.Bg5 Nc8; 26.Qb7 hxg3; 27.Nxg3 e4; 28.Ra8 Be5; 29.Bh6.** 29.Nf1!? might have been considered. **29...Rf7.** The time for patience is over. Having successfully infiltrated the enemy position, the next task is to rip pieces off the board and achieve an endgame in which the queenside advantage, specifically Black's weakness at b6, is sufficient for a win. **30.Rxc8+ Kh7.** The position has grown very complicated, but I simply and patiently pursue the goal of exchanging queens.

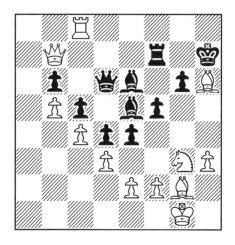

31.Bf8! Rxb7; 32.Bxd6 Bxg3; 33.Rc6 Bxd6; 34.Rxd6.
The endgame is tremendous for White. The pawn chains are anchored at the very defensible e2 and f2 squares for White, but at the weak b6 and g6 squares in the Black camp.
34...Bf7; 35.Kh2 Rb8; 36.Rd7 Kg8; 37.h4 Ra8; 38.Rb7 Ra2. Black has now taken the a-file and performed his own infiltration, but the struggle has shifted to the center, where White remains superior. **39.dxe4 Rxe2; 40.exf5 Rxf2; 41.Rxb6.** The base of the pawn chain finally falls. White's b-pawn, already well advanced, now has just a few squares to go to reach the promotion square.

GAME LESSON FORTY-SIX
Games involving big chains of pawns require patient pursuit of the base of the pawn chain.

Bxc4; 42.Rxg6+ Kf7; 43.b6 Ba6; 44.Kg3 Rxf5; 45.Rc6 Kg7; 46.Rc7+ Rf7; 47.Ra7 d3. Too late. Black cannot survive. **48.Rxa6.** I took the simple road. But there was another, better win: 48.Bd5 Rxa7; 49.bxa7 d2; 50.a8Q d1Q; 51.Qg8+ Kh6; 52.Qf8+ Kg6; 53.Be4+ Kh5; 54.Qh8#.

48...d2; 49.Ra1 c4; 50.Be4 c3; 51.Bc2 Rf6; 52.Rb1 Rf8; 53.b7. Black resigned.

PATIENCE! - B

Since the Reti had been serving me well, with its slow approach to the opening, I decided to keep using it against Grandmasters. Patience is essential to that opening strategy, which is why it probably didn't serve me well in my younger years.

1.Nf3 d5; 2.c4 d4; 3.g3 g6; 4.b4 Bg7; 5.Bb2 e5; 6.d3 a5; 7.b5 Ne7; 8.Bg2 0–0; 9.0–0. As in the game with Gurevich, I grab as much territory as I can on the queenside.

9...c5! A clever defense. If I do not capture, giving up my prized b-pawn, then the queenside will remain closed and the base of the pawn chain, soon to be at b6, will remain forever out of reach.

Position after 9...c5

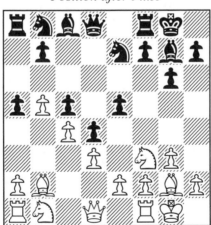

Schiller vs. Yakovich, New York Open, 1998

10.bxc6 Nexc6; 11.Nbd2 Na6; 12.Ne1 Be6; 13.Nc2 Qd7.
Black wins the development race, but must have some concerns over the semi-open b-file. There is nothing much White can

do at the moment, but by patiently increasing pressure on the queenside the game will become difficult to play for Black.

14.Ba3 Rfd8; 15.Rb1 Rab8; 16.Ne4 h6; 17.Nc5.

My knight on e4 certainly seemed stronger than the enemy knight at a6, but Black could easily drive my knight back and the enemy knight did have control of the important b4-square. Call it an even trade, in an even position.

17...Nxc5; 18.Bxc5 Bh3; 19.Rb5. Preparing to put as much pressure as possible on the pawn at b7. Black will be able to defend, but that will divert resources from other squares.

19...Bxg2; 20.Kxg2 Re8; 21.Qb1 e4. Black is trying to weaken the base of my pawn chain by exchanging at d3. Since I control the e3-square, and Black doesn't have a light-squared bishop, my pawn at d3 will not be easily captured.

22.Bb6 exd3; 23.exd3 Re5.

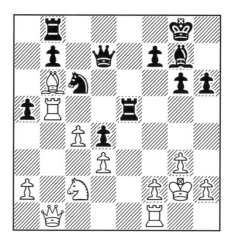

This is no time for nervous play. Black has no real threats and the bishop at g7 has no influence. Time to calmly decide which pieces should be removed from the board. I decide to eliminate all the rooks. Although this gives me less pressure at b7, I can concentrate on the weak pawn at a5 as well.

24.Re1! Rbe8; 25.Rbxe5 Rxe5; 26.Rxe5 Nxe5. White has to be a little careful about the weaknesses of the light squares, and especially the a8-h1 diagonal.

27.Qb5! Qg4. 27...Qxb5; 28.cxb5 Nxd3; 29.Bxd4 didn't really come into consideration. This was round 1, and the Grandmaster wasn't going to let me off with an easy draw!

28.Nxd4 Nxd3; 29.Qe8+ Bf8. The game is still even, which means my opponent was feeling the pressure of trying to defeat a lower-ranked opponent.

30.Qe3.

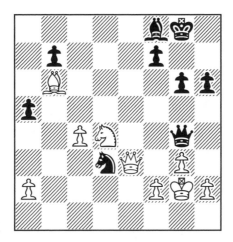

This move contains a trap, which my opponent did not manage to avoid. The knight should retreat to b4 and then to c6 if I attack it with my pawn. I can't win the a-pawn in this line without losing one of my own pawns.

GAME LESSON FORTY-SEVEN

When facing a superior opponent, use slow patient play until you spot favorable tactical operations.

30...Bc5?? In growing time pressure, and after being under considerable pressure on the queenside, Black blunders. **31.Bxc5 Nxc5; 32.Qe8+ Kg7; 33.Qe5+.** The knight at c5 falls, so Black resigned.

DEEEE-FENSE!

When you are facing a strong opponent, you have to expect that over the course of the first thirty moves or so you'll often find yourself defending a difficult position. As we've seen in many previous examples, the attacking side has the advantage of not necessarily needing to find the best moves.

The defender, on the other hand, cannot afford a mistake. Defensive thinking requires paying attention to all threats and potential threats. As long as you can keep parrying the enemy thrusts you will be able to hold off the attack.

One of the great dangers faced by the defending side is the tendency to overestimate a threat. The thought of an enemy piece invading the position is a frightening one. Still, if it is just a single piece you may not have much to worry about. Perhaps the worst case of a single-piece invasion is an enemy queen at h7 after you have castled kingside.

If the rook hasn't moved, and the queen is defended, that's going to be checkmate. If, however, an escape route is prepared via f8 and e7, and the e-file is closed, the invasion may be nothing more than a minor annoyance. In the best case, the queen will even find herself offside!

1.d4 d5; 2.c4 e6; 3.Nc3 c5; 4.e3.

My opponent is a veteran Grandmaster and has always preferred a classical and quiet approach to the White side of the Queen's Gambit.

4...Nf6; 5.Nf3 a6.

A particular favorite of mine, because it unbalances the pawn structure and breaks the symmetry.

Here is the early opening position:

Position after 5...a6

Bisguier vs. Schiller, World Open, Philadelphia, 1986

6.cxd5 cxd4; 7.exd4 Nxd5. A typical isolated d-pawn position, with Black securely blockading the d5-square. **8.Bd3 Nc6; 9.0–0 Be7; 10.Re1 Bf6; 11.Ne4 h6; 12.Bc2 0–0; 13.Nxf6+ Qxf6; 14.Qd3.** The queen aims at h7, hoping to deliver a checkmate. **14...Rd8!; 15.Be3 Kf8.** I am preparing for the invasion at h7 by opening up an escape route via e7. **16.Rac1 Bd7; 17.Bb3 Be8; 18.Qh7.** The queen invades, threatening a nasty check at h8. **18...Nce7.** My king is now shut in, but the knight can come to g8 and the minor pieces and pawns offer plenty of defense.

The bishop can now use c6 as a temporary home to block the c-file, adding to the security of the king.

19.Bd2 a5; 20.Ne5 Bc6; 21.Bxd5 Rxd5; 22.Re3.

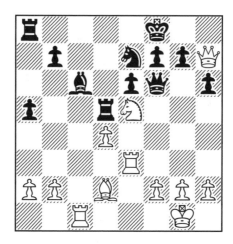

White is preparing the killer move Rf3, so I must clear the path for my bishop. I grab the d-pawn, knowing that it will cost me the exchange. In return, my bishop comes alive and f3 will be unavailable to White.

22...Rxd4; 23.Bc3. Obviously I dare not move this rook.

23...Rad8; 24.Bxd4 Rxd4; 25.Qh8+ Ng8; 26.Nxc6 bxc6; 27.Rb3.

Again the future looks bleak, but I have a saving resource. White's queen can never return to the game, so all I have to do is neutralize the immediate threat.

27...Qf4! This covers b8 while attacking c1.

28.Rf1 Qd6!; 29.h3 Rd1. I now eliminate a pair of rooks while increasing the power of my queen. **30.Rxd1 Qxd1+; 31.Kh2 Qd6+; 32.g3 Qd4!**

GAME LESSON FORTY-EIGHT

An invading queen is a formidable force, but she can't beat you all by herself!

The knight at g8 is not important if I can establish a perpetual check at f2. **33.Kg2 Qd5+; 34.Rf3 Qe4; 35.g4 f6; 36.Kg3.** Black is certainly no worse, but I agreed to the draw.

AN UNUSUAL STALEMATE

Stalemate themes are common in endgames. Normally, the king finds himself stalemated with his back to the edge of the board. Stalemating a king in the center is usually the property of composers of chess problems. In the next game, a very unusual stalemate is created, right in the middle of the board!

Position after 38...Rf3

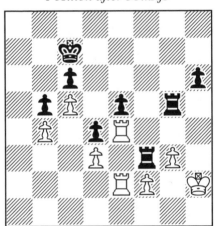

Macaulay vs. Schiller, Wightman Cup final
London, 1982

Black is in great difficulty here but the last move, played just before the game was adjourned, provides a small initiative. The strategy, worked out over the one week interval by the King's Head team headed by Jon Speelman, with Ray Keene and Jon Tisdall among others, managed to hold the draw, and win the championship as a result.

Speelman came up with the fantasy stalemate idea, and I found a pawn sacrifice that made it happen. **39.Rd2!;** 39.Rxe5 Rxe5; 40.Rxe5 Rxf2+ is even.

39...Rgf5; 40.Kg2 h5! played to prevent g4, but also part of a deep plan. **41.Rh4.** This leads to the win of a pawn. **41... Kd7; 42.Rxh5 Rxh5!!** 42...Rxf2+?; 43.Rxf2 Rxh5; 44.Rf6 is crushing. **43.Kxf3 Rh1.** Black threatens to circle around to win the b-pawn, forcing White to react vigorously.

44.Kg4 Ke6; 45.Re2 Kd5.

Black's king will now be in a stalemate position if the e-pawn is removed. **46.Kf5.** The point is shown in the variation 46.f4 exf4; 47.gxf4 Rh4+!!; 48.Kf5 Rxf4+!; 49.Kxf4. Stalemate! **46...Rh5+; 47.Kf6 Rh6+; 48.Kf5 Rh5+.** The game was eventually drawn.

GAME LESSON FORTY-NINE

When your endgame looks sick, try to find a stalemate trick!

ENDGAME TECHNIQUE - A

The previous game was a most unusual one. In the following games we will see more generally applicable endgame strategies. The examples here are instructive because they show that if you understand which inferior endgames are drawable, you can escape even from very strong players.

Some players are afraid to enter inferior endgames, lacking confidence in their own endgame skills and often overestimating those of the opponent. If the position can be held, it is your obligation to hold it. As long as you don't make a mistake, a half point is yours for the taking. Easier said than done!

Position after 24.Bf1

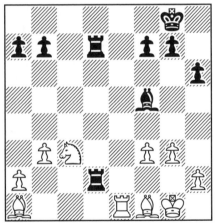

Levitt vs. Schiller, London, 1981

24...Bd3! What is Black doing trying to exchange, when White will have a material advantage in the endgame? This is a typical Tarrasch Defense plan, counting on activity to compensate for material. In the end, White is often better, but the advantage is insufficient to win.

GAME LESSON FIFTY

An invasion of the seventh rank ties down enemy
forces and can compensate for minor material
diadvantage.

25.a4. 25.Bh3 would have been stronger, but White doesn't
think the exchange of bishops will hurt. **25...Bxf1; 26.Rxf1
Rc2.** A rook on the seventh is so powerful with exposed rim
pawns that White is almost paralyzed.
27.Ne4 Rd3; 28.b4. White offered a draw, and I accepted.
We agreed afterwards that Black was at least equal here.

ENDGAME TECHNIQUE - B

Grandmaster Jansa helped me analyze this difficult rook
and pawn endgame. We had adjourned games to look at almost
every round! The hours of study in the evening really contributed
to my knowledge of endgames. I miss adjournments, though
I understand that computers have rendered them a bit less
sporting. Still, you learn so much from analyzing, especially
with others.

Position after 41.Kd2

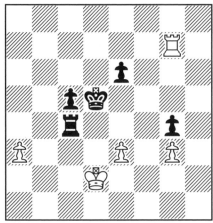

*Schiller vs. Einarsson, Gausdal International
Norway, 1984*

Most of my friends figured this position was hopelessly lost, but it wasn't so simple. **41...Ra4; 42.Ke2 e5; 43.Rg6 Rxa3; 44.Rxg4 Ra2+.** 44... c4 would have given me more trouble. On 45.Rg8 Ra2+; 46.Kf3 c3; 47.Rd8+ Kc4; 48.Ke4 Ra5; 49.Rc8+ Kb3; 50.Rb8+ Kc2; 51.g4, or 48...c2; 49.Rc8+ Kb3; 50.Kd3 e4+; 51.Kd2, Black can't win unless White makes a serious mistake. **45.Kd3 e4+; 46.Kc3 Ra3+; 47.Kd2 Ra2+; 48.Kc3 Ra3+; 49.Kd2 Rd3+; 50.Ke2.** The reason for all this fooling around is that we were headed toward yet another adjournment session, when both players could get some more lessons from our Grandmaster friends! **50...Rb3; 51.Kd2 Rb1; 52.Kc2 Rf1; 53.Kd2 Rf3; 54.Ke2 Rf5; 55.Rg8 Re5; 56.g4 Kc4; 57.g5.**

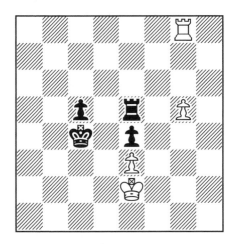

Here the game was adjourned again, but a draw is going to be inevitable. Still, we each got an additional lesson out of it, but of course agreed to a draw quickly the next morning after **57...Kc3; 58.g6 Rg5.**

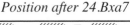

GAME LESSON FIFTY-ONE

Study endgames with the experts and you'll learn as much as you can absorb!

ENDGAME TECHNIQUE - C

Even with bishops of the same color, the following endgame may not be winnable. Both sides were in time trouble, with control at move 30. International Master Walter Shipman has a well-deserved reputation for persistence in the endgame, so I knew I was in for a fight.

Position after 24.Bxa7

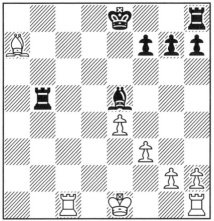

Shipman vs. Schiller, Golden Bear Class Struggle
Berkeley, 1998

24...0–0; 25.0–0 Ra8; 26.Bf2 h5. Black tries to set up a drawn rook and four vs. rook and three pawn structure, hoping to exchange bishops and a pair of rooks later. **27.Rc5.** I was quite pleased to see White cooperate, but there wasn't much choice as otherwise Black might soon double rooks on the seventh rank.

27...Rxc5; 28.Bxc5 Ra2; 29.Rd1 g6; 30.Rd8+ Kg7.

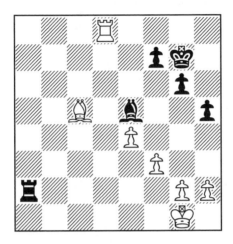

Time control is reached. White can exchange bishops, but that leads to a technical, if very complicated, draw. This pure rook endgame has been analyzed by several World Champions, and fortunately I had studied it in detail. Black has the ideal defensive position. **31.g3 Rc2; 32.Bf2 h4!** The threat of ...h3 forces White's hand. **33.gxh4** or 33.Bd4 Bxd4+; 34.Rxd4 h3 is no problem for Black. **33...Bxh2+; 34.Kf1.** 34.Kxh2 Rxf2+; 35.Kg3 Rf1 should also end in a draw. **34...Be5; 35.Rd5 Kf6; 36.Be3 Ke6.**

Black's pieces are ideally posted, and now that there is a weakness in White's kingside pawn structure a draw is likely. The sudden death time control encouraged further play. **37.Ra5 Rh2; 38.Ra6+ Kd7!; 39.Bf2.** An attempt to trap the rook. **39...Rh1+; 40.Ke2 Rh2; 41.Ke3?** Hardly the best way to play for a win as the bishops now come off. **41...Bd4+!; 42.Kxd4 Rxf2; 43.Rf6.** The rook must defend the f-pawn and h-pawn. **43...Ke7; 44.Ke5 Rh2.**

Here I offered a draw, though I know that IM Shipman almost always plays on in an endgame where he has any advantage, real or imagined. White cannot win against accurate defense, and in fact it is even possible to exchange the two Black pawns for White's e-pawn and still have a drawn position.

45.Rf4 Rh3; 46.Kd4 Rg3; 47.Ke3 Rg1; 48.Rg4 Ra1; 49.Kf4 Rh1; 50.Kg5 Ra1; 51.f4 Ra8; 52.f5 gxf5. But not 52...f6+? since 53.Kh6 gxf5; 54.exf5 Rh8+; 55.Kg7 Rh5; 56.Rf4 wins. **53.Kxf5 Rh8; 54.Rf4 Rh5+; 55.Kg4 Rh8; 56.h5 f6; 57.Rf5 Ke6; 58.Ra5 Rg8+; 59.Kh4 Rh8; 60.Ra7 Ke5.**

The sudden death period was running out, and the remaining moves were made very quickly. **61.Re7+ Kf4; 62.Re6 f5; 63.exf5.** 63.e5 gets nowhere after 63...Rg8; 64.h6 Rg4+; 65.Kh3 Rg1. **63...Kxf5; 64.Rg6 Ra8.** Draw agreed.

GAME LESSON FIFTY-TWO

Know the four pawns against three pawns kingside rook endgame, as it is especially useful in fast time controls!

ENDGAME TECHNIQUE - D

As is usually the case in my games with Grandmaster Bisguier, he gets a slight endgame advantage. However, over the years I have improved my endgame play to the point where I can hold my own. My queenside pawn structure is weak. I must not give in to temptation and swap bishops. Instead, I have to aim for an endgame in which my pawn structure is repaired. Therefore I must wait and let my opponent exchange pieces at b3.

Position after 25.Nxd3

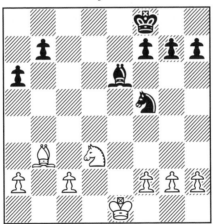

Schiller vs. Bisguier, American Open, Los Angeles, 1995

25...Nd4; 26.Nc5 Bc8; 27.Kd2 Nxb3+; 28.cxb3. I knew this endgame structure. With balanced, symmetrical pawns and three open files in the center, the knight can be effective enough to hold the draw. The rest is just a matter of Black's frustrated attempts to make progress.

GAME LESSON FIFTY-THREE

Keep the knight in the center in the endgame, so that it can move to either flank as required.

28...Ke7; 29.Kc3 Kd6; 30.Kd4 h6; 31.Ne4+ Kc6; 32.Ng3 Kb5; 33.Ne4. Centralizing the knight.

33...Kc6; 34.Ng3 a5; 35.Nh5 g6; 36.Nf4 b5; 37.Nd3 Be; 38.b4 axb4; 39.Nxb4+ Kb6; 40.a3 Ka5; 41.Kc3 Ka4; 42.Kb2 Bc4; 43.Nc6 Bd5; 44.Ne5 b4; 45.axb4 Kxb4; 46.f3. Agreed Drawn.

ENDGAME TECHNIQUE - E

Our final example displays the lesson that confidence plays in the endgame. Many players would fear entering an endgame down a pawn in an open position where the enemy also has the advantage of bishop vs. knight. If you know which pawn structures are defensible, you can enter such endgames with decent prospects of earning a draw.

Position after 37.Bd1

Annakov vs. Schiller, National Open, Las Vegas, 2000

Not a pleasant sight, especially when your opponent is rated over 2600! My opponent has bishop against knight, a pawn advantage, and advanced pawns on the flanks. But the advanced queenside pawns are also a bit weak. I had just exchanged rooks at d1, a decision that gave me greater drawing chances, as otherwise the rook and bishop tag team is much better than rook and knight, never mind the pawn.

My decision was correct. Even though Black also suffers from a weak pawn at h6, White just doesn't have enough to create an easy win. Perhaps with 100% correct play White can prevail. The burden on my opponent is tremendous, while I just have to avoid weakening my position further and pay close attention to the queenside.

To begin with, I mustn't allow White to get to b6 first, because I have to get the pawn off the light square at b7. **37...b6; 38.axb6 axb6; 39.Kh2.** Since I have eliminated any bishop threats by placing my pawns on the squares of the opposite color as the bishop, White starts the journey toward the pawn at h6. The pawn at b5 can be defended by a bishop when needed, and if the Black king wanders queenside, then the kingside pawns fall, and White can sacrifice the bishop for the b-pawn if it even gets near b1. **39...Ke7; 40.Kg3 Nd5.**

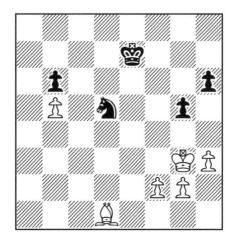

41.Bf3?! 41.Be2 Nc3; 42.Bf1!? was a better plan. Grandmaster Annakov didn't see the point of my defensive plan yet. By the time he did, it was too late!

GAME LESSON FIFTY-FOUR

Don't assume you can't hold an inferior endgame, play as if you are invincible!

41...Nc3; 42.Kg4. The only try. 42.Bc6 doesn't work, though deep analysis is needed. 42...Ne2+; 43.Kg4 Nd4; 44.Kh5 Nxc6; 45.Kxh6! Nd4; 46.Kxg5 where White will just manage to draw thanks to the kingside pawns. 46...Nxb5; 47.h4 Nd6; 48.Kf4 b5; 49.Ke5 b4; 50.Kd4 Kf6; 51.g4 etc.

42...Nxb5; 43.Kh5 Kf6; 44.Kxh6 Nd4! This is what I had been playing for.

45.Be4 b5; 46.Kh5 b4; 47.h4. There is nothing better. 47...gxh4; 48.Kxh4 b3; **49.g4?** 49.Bd3 keeps the game level. The move played in the game forces a draw. **49...Ke5!; 50.Bd3**

Kf4! Draw agreed, as there is no way to advance the pawns. If g5, then ...Nf3+. Black can't win because White can always sacrifice the bishop for the pawn.

♟ STEP SEVEN
Final Thoughts

I hope you have learned from my mistakes! My lessons were often painful ones, and trust me, you'd rather not learn the hard way. Nevertheless, even if you do manage to avoid the pitfalls you've encountered in this book, there are plenty of other traps lying hidden in all stages of the game. In order to make progress, you have to honestly evaluate your play and identify all of your mistakes. That way you can hope you won't repeat them, at least not too often.

In writing this book I was fortunate in having access to a lot of notes scribbled in the margins of my scoresheets. When you do a post-mortem on your game, preferably with your opponent right after the game, try to take notice of the key lines and most interesting variations. Then you can review the position at home, perhaps with the aid of a chess program.

It is only natural, after a loss, to try to chase the game from your mind as if it were a ferocious demon. That's why it is important to review the game once again, after the pain has subsided and objectivity returns. Just as films and tapes are used in sports to dissect performance, you must use your scoresheet as a fountain of knowledge, not as a reminder of a painful past.

I recommend noting the time used for each move (or at least every few moves) during the game. This can help remind you if an error was made in haste, or, as strangely often seems to be the case, after an extended period of thinking.

The most important thing is to hang on to your scoresheets. The cold binary bits of computers can hold a list of moves, but your scoresheets can reveal much more. In my case, you can easily see where I lose confidence in any chance of survival, as my handwriting disintegrates. If you write down moves before you play them, the number of scratch-outs or erasures can point you to positions in which you experienced some difficulty, even when reviewed years later.

This advice is practical even for beginners. An instructor can help a lot more when you can supply a set of games that show your weaknesses, and of course having scoresheets means you can also triumphantly put your best efforts on display.

I wish I had records of many more games that I recall as instructive but where the scoresheet was either lost, or destroyed (accidentally, or in some cases, in a fit of rage!). Keep your games and study them well, so you can learn from your own mistakes. After all, I don't intend to leave behind an inexhaustible supply!

GAME LESSON FIFTY-FIVE

Treasure your losses as you do your wins, and they may wind up bringing you even greater rewards in the long run!

OPPONENTS INDEX

(Numbers refer to Game Lessons, not page numbers)

3 1170 00830 0620

192